# FOREIGN DIRECT INVESTMENT

Ownership Advantages, Firm Specific Factors,
Survival and Performance

# FOREIGN DIRECT INVESTMENT

## Ownership Advantages, Firm Specific Factors, Survival and Performance

### Mehdi Rasouli Ghahroudi
University of St. Gallen, Switzerland

### Yasuo Hoshino
University of Tsukuba, Japan

### Stephen Turnbull
University of Tsukuba, Japan

 **World Scientific**

NEW JERSEY · LONDON · SINGAPORE · BEIJING · SHANGHAI · HONG KONG · TAIPEI · CHENNAI · TOKYO

*Published by*

World Scientific Publishing Co. Pte. Ltd.

5 Toh Tuck Link, Singapore 596224

*USA office:* 27 Warren Street, Suite 401-402, Hackensack, NJ 07601

*UK office:* 57 Shelton Street, Covent Garden, London WC2H 9HE

**Library of Congress Cataloging-in-Publication Data**

Names: Rasouli Ghahroudi, Mehdi, author. | Hoshino, Yasuo, author. | Turnbull, Stephen, author.
Title: Foreign direct investment : ownership advantages, firm specific factors, survival and
    performance / by Mehdi Rasouli Ghahroudi, Yasuo Hoshino and Stephen Turnbull.
Description: New Jersey : World Scientific, [2019] | Includes bibliographical references.
Identifiers: LCCN 2018022443 | ISBN 9789813238398
Subjects: LCSH: Investments, Foreign. | International business enterprises.
Classification: LCC HG4538 .G43 2019 | DDC 332.67/3--dc23
LC record available at https://lccn.loc.gov/2018022443

**British Library Cataloguing-in-Publication Data**

A catalogue record for this book is available from the British Library.

For any available supplementary material, please visit
https://www.worldscientific.com/worldscibooks/10.1142/10942#t=suppl

Desk Editor: Lum Pui Yee

Typeset by Stallion Press
Email: enquiries@stallionpress.com

Printed in Singapore

# Preface

This book extends the literature in FDI by providing empirical support for several theories and previously defined and tested constructs.

The purpose of this study was to extend and develop the literature on foreign investment and multinational corporation (MNCs) subsidiaries. There are several reasons for studying foreign investment and ownership. First, firms need to identify which host country industry factors are important in choosing among the various type of equity ownership (e.g. international joint ventures or wholly-owned subsidiary). Second, international diversification through foreign market entry can provide growth and profitability at rates unavailable in home markets. A third reason this warrants some attention is that type of ownership can affect attempts to counter international competition by engaging foreign rivals on their home turf. Fourth, firms have the option of choosing the appropriate equity ownership for international markets based on balancing their resources, capabilities and international experience with their desire for ownership and control.

Foreign direct investment (FDI) is very important to any national economy. While it is possible to survive using only funds generated from within one's own borders, this type of isolationism can too often have a negative impact on the growth prospects of the country. Although it is not the governments themselves that directly receive the funds, a stronger business economy is a boon to governments as it promises more jobs, a higher standard of living, and a greater tax base. And though target companies are under great scrutiny as far as profitability, growth, and potential are concerned, national factors such as country risk, political stability and population and gross national product (GNP) growth can be deciding factors for investing companies (Dunning, 1998).

Host countries often take an interest in increasing domestic participation in the benefits of foreign investment. But the reduction of foreign equity through legislation or persuasion is an expensive and lengthy process, and outright expropriation risks an investment boycott and backlash from the foreign investors' home countries, imposition of domestic equity requirements at the stage of entry of the foreign firms through the process of investment approval is the more popular approach.

Yet many countries have been dismantling such controls in the past two decades. Developing countries, emerging economies and countries in transition have come increasingly to see FDI as a source of economic development and modernization, income growth and employment. Countries have liberalized their foreign investment regimes and pursued other policies to attract investment. They have addressed the issue of how best to pursue domestic policies to maximize the benefits of foreign presence in the domestic economy. The study of foreign investment attempts primarily to shed light on the second issue, by focusing on the overall effect of foreign investment on macroeconomic growth and other welfare enhancing processes, and on the channels through which these benefits take effect. But some of our findings are consistent with the position that liberalization has been effective in attracting foreign capital, though at the expense of conceding greater control of enterprises to MNCs.

Findings in this book offer a number of contributions to the literature. First, there are very few studies about foreign investment in India which has recently experienced superlative economic growth for a developing country. Second, most other studies focused on subsidiaries established in developed and Asian developing countries by focusing on one host country and foreign investment outflow of a single country, while our research covered foreign investment and MNCs from several home countries in Japan. Third, we adopt an integrative approach, which incorporates knowledge transfer factors, parent firm and subsidiary firm variables. Fourth, we employ a multidimensional measure of performance which enables us to examine subsidiary performance determinants at different views. Fifth, our findings reveal that impacts of explanatory variables are different on various dimensions of performance. Few studies have attempted to use such multidimensional measures, including sales growth and asset growth as well as survival of subsidiaries.

The choice of research site, Japan, is appropriate on several grounds. First, Japan is the world's second largest national economy; secondly, Japan is an important source of foreign investment research and Japanese foreign investment has an one of the largest FDI outflows in the world especially to South Asia and East Asian countries; and thirdly, there are very few studies in FDI research area focusing on foreign affiliated companies in Japan.

This study provides empirical support for several theories and previously defined and/or tested constructs. For example, the parent and subsidiary's factors measured in this study suggest the importance of internalization and ownership advantages of Dunning's eclectic theory. However, according to resource-based theory, the number of employees, capital and total assets constructs measured in this study propose the effect of a firm's resources on performance and ownership of foreign affiliates.

Findings in the book show that foreign affiliates with higher levels of control and experience in host market have better performance. MNCs prefer to acquire higher levels of control for larger subsidiaries. It shows that transaction costs play a very important role in the finding of an efficient and successful market entry strategy. When transaction costs increase, MNCs tend to switch to more hierarchical modes such as wholly-owned subsidiaries. In recent periods, Japanese MNCs prefer to acquire high levels of equity ownership, up to full ownership, especially when the subsidiary is in the manufacturing industry. Finally, smaller subsidiaries are likely to have superior growth and higher survival rates.

The research in this book also examines firm-specific factors and foreign affiliate performance based on data derived from 3500 affiliates of MNCs in Japan. The findings show that the factors of industry, foreign employees and the size, generate a significant effect on performance. The research indicates that foreign affiliates with greater ratio of foreign ownership are more likely to develop and transfer the knowledge in management and employees levels from parent companies. However, consistent with resource-based theory, the findings demonstrate the effects of firm resources on ownership and performance of foreign affiliates.

The study find that the factors of foreign ownership, experience in host market, country of origin, export ratio, parent company sales and firm size affect performance. Finally, firms with higher equity of ownership and those in manufacturing industry have superior import ratio. According to transaction cost theory, when a company decides whether to outsource or to produce goods or services on its own, market prices are not the sole factor. However, there are also other factors such as transaction costs, search costs, contracting costs and coordination costs. These costs often determine whether a company uses internal or external resources for its manufacturing or service activities.

The book starts with this introduction to the focus, objectives and contributions of this book. After the first theory chapter, the next three chapters present the main research analyses, and their findings. Chapter 2 explores the relationship between age and entry strategies of wholly-owned vs. joint venture companies. We examine the effects of equity ownership, size, entry strategy and subsidiary age on the sales growth ratio and subsidiary's survival, using a data for Japanese firms investing in India. Chapter 3 uses a data set on inward FDI to Japan, and examines first the impact of knowledge transfer factors, parent firm specific factors and subsidiary characteristics on foreign affiliated performance. Second, it throws light on the relationship between firm specific factors and the foreign ownership ratio. Chapter 4 explores the relationship between type of industry and subsidiary age, export ratio and parent-specific factors, using the same data set as Chapter 3. We also examined the impact of country of origin, foreign ownership and parent's specific factors on asset growth ratio.

Chapter 5 summarizes the researches in the context of the literature and presents the overall conclusions and implications of the researches; and explains the limitations associated with the analyses and results.

# About the Authors

**Dr. Mehdi Rasouli Ghahroudi** is an Assistant Professor at the Institute for Management and Planning Studies (IMPS). He received his doctorate degree in international business from "University of Tsukuba". He was a post-doctoral researcher at the "University of St. Gallen" for 2 years. Dr. Rasouli's research interests focuses on international management, FDI, commercialization, export performance, family business, SMEs, corporate governance and international marketing. He has working experience in several companies in various industries as a sales and marketing manager. He also has been an active consultant in marketing, branding, international financing and investment, business plan and feasibility studies as well as strategic management.

**Dr. Yasuo Hoshino** is a Professor Emeritus at the University of Tsukuba, Tsukuba, Japan and Visiting Fellow at Aichi University, Nagoya, Japan. He is a consultant at Japan Federation of Management and the Union of National Economic Association in Japan. He is Managing Editor of "Japanese Journal of Administrative Science", and Associate Editor of "Review of Pacific Basin Financial Markets and Policies", "Journal of Financial Management and

Analysis", "SMART Journal of Business Management Studies", "Modern Economy" and others. He has published 121 articles, more than half of which are written in refereed English journals and 29 books, of which 19 are written in English.

 **Dr. Stephen Turnbull** is an Associate Professor in the Faculty of Engineering, Information and Systems of the University of Tsukuba. His primary research interests include strategy and the software and Internet industries. His interest in international business studies arose from the need for internationalized software in a bilingual research and educational environment, and from there to the business issues involved in internationalizing IT operations which naturally arise in multinational business activity.

# Acknowledgments

This Book is dedicated to my wife Saharnaz and my son Dana. Special thanks go to my dear parents Gholamreza and Narges and my sisters and brothers. My family have stayed with me over the past years and encouraged me in so many ways. Some encouraged me to continue in desperate times, and others willingly listened to my little problems or stories. I appreciate their unconditional love and continuous support and I hope to enjoy it for many more years. I would like to extend my thanks to my Professors and my academic advisers for their understanding, support and helpful guidance during this study. Their kind gestures will neverbe forgotten.

Mehdi Rasouli Ghahroudi

This study is supported by JSPS KAKENHI Grant Number 13630133.

Yasuo Hoshino

I thank my family for their patience during the editing of this book, and my co-authors for fascinating discussions and their willingness to make many pedantic changes to satisfy my very particular sense of style.

Stephen J. Turnbull

# Contents

*Preface*                                                                v

*About the Authors*                                                     ix

*Acknowledgments*                                                       xi

**Chapter 1   Introduction**                                            **1**
    1.1.  Introduction                               1
    1.2.  Reasons to Study FDI                       2
    1.3.  FDI and MNCs                               3
    1.4.  Research in FDI                            7

**Chapter 2   A Review of Theories of Multinational Enterprises**       **11**
    2.1.  Introduction                               11
    2.2.  The industrial organization theory         12
    2.3.  The internalization theory                 13
    2.4.  The location theory                       14
    2.5.  The eclectic theory (OLI paradigm)        16
    2.6.  The product life cycle theory             19
    2.7.  The internal financing hypothesis         21
    2.8.  The Kojima theory                         22
    2.9.  Theories of entry modes                   22
    2.10. The classical theory of corporate governance  25
    2.11. Agency theory                             26

2.12. Transaction cost theory                                    26
2.13. Resource-based theory                                      29
2.14. Stages models of internationalization                      31
2.15. Monopolistic advantage theory                              32

**Chapter 3   Entry Strategies and Survival of MNC's
Subsidiaries**                                                   **45**
   3.1. Introduction                              45
   3.2. Theoretical background and hypotheses     47
   3.3. Research design and methodology            52
      3.3.1. Sample and data collection   52
      3.3.2. Description and measurement of variables   53
   3.4. Empirical analysis and discussion          55
   3.5. Conclusions and limitations                64

**Chapter 4   Foreign Ownership, Knowledge Transfer
and Parent Firm Specificity**                                    **67**
   4.1. Introduction                              67
   4.2. Theoretical background and hypotheses     69
      4.2.1. Knowledge transfer     69
      4.2.2. Ownership advantages   73
      4.2.3. Parent firm-specific   74
      4.2.4. Subsidiary firm-specific   76
   4.3. Research design and methodology            78
      4.3.1. Sample and data collection   78
      4.3.2. Description and measurement
      of variables                   83
   4.4. Empirical analysis and discussion          87
   4.5. Conclusion and limitations                102

**Chapter 5   Industry, Firm-specific Factors and Performance**   **105**
   5.1. Introduction                              105
   5.2. Theoretical background and hypotheses     107
      5.2.1. Industry and firms factors   107
      5.2.2. Asset growth           110

5.3. Research design and methodology 114
    5.3.1. Sample and data collection 114
    5.3.2. Description and measurement
        of variables 116
5.4. Empirical analysis and discussion 120
5.5. Conclusion and limitations 127

**Chapter 6**   **Conclusions**     **131**

*References*     141

*Index*     161

# Chapter 1

# Introduction

## 1.1. Introduction

Foreign direct investment (FDI) is the process whereby residents of one country (the source country) acquire ownership of assets in another country (the host country) for the purpose of controlling the production, distribution and other activities of a firm in that country.

UNCTAD, 1999 defines FDI as "an investment involving a long-term relationship and reflecting a lasting interest and control of a resident entity in one economy (foreign direct investor or parent enterprise) in an enterprise resident in an economy other than that of the foreign direct investor (FDI enterprise, affiliate enterprise or foreign affiliate)." The term "long-term" is used in the last definition in order to distinguish FDI from portfolio investment, the latter characterized by being short-term in nature and involving a high turnover of securities.

The distinguishing feature of FDI, in comparison with other forms of international investment, is the element of control over management policy and decisions. Razin *et al.* (1999) argue that the element of control gives direct investors an informational advantage over foreign portfolio investors and over domestic savers. Many firms are unwilling to carry out foreign investment unless they have 100% equity ownership and control. Others refuse to make such investments unless they have at least majority control (that is, a 51% stake). In recent years, however, there has been a tendency to indulge in cooperative FDI arrangements, where several firms participate and no single party holds majority control (for example, joint ventures).

The term "control" implies that some degree of discretionary decision-making by the investor is present in management policies and strategy. For example, this control may occur through the ability of the investor to elect or select one or more members on the board of directors of the foreign company or foreign subsidiary. It is even possible to distinguish between the control market for shares and the non-control or portfolio share market as an analogy to the distinction between direct investment and portfolio investment. It may be possible to exercise control via contractual (non-equity) arrangements. The non-equity forms of FDI include, inter alia, subcontracting, management contracts, franchising, licensing and product sharing (Moosa, 2002). Lall and Streeten (1977) argue that a majority shareholding is not a necessary condition for exercising control, as it may be achievable with a low equity share and even without an explicit management contract.

## 1.2. Reasons to Study FDI

Interest in FDI, which has motivated attempts to come up with theories that explain its causes and effects, is attributed to the following factors. The first is the rapid growth in FDI and the change in its pattern, particularly since the 1980s. In the 1990s, FDI accounted for about a quarter of international capital outflows, having grown relative to other forms of international investment since the 1970s. The rapid growth of FDI has resulted from global competition as well as from the tendency to free up financial, goods and factor markets. It has been observed that FDI flows continue to expand even when world trade slows down. It has also been observed that even when portfolio investment dried up in Asian countries as a result of the crisis of the 1990s, FDI flows were not affected significantly (Moosa, 2002).

The second reason for interest in FDI is the concern it raises about the causes and consequences of foreign ownership. The views on this issue are so diverse, falling between the extreme of regarding FDI as symbolizing new colonialism or imperialism, and the other extreme of viewing it as something without which the host country cannot survive. Most countries show an ambivalent attitude towards FDI. Inward FDI is said to have negative employment effects, retard home-grown technological progress, and worsen the trade balance. A substantial foreign ownership often gives rise to concern about the loss of sovereignty and compromise of national security. Outward FDI is sometimes blamed for the export of employment, and for giving foreigners access to domestic technology.

The third reason for studying FDI is that it offers the possibility for channeling resources to developing countries. According to this argument, FDI is becoming an important source of funds at a time when access to other means of financing is dwindling, particularly in the aftermath of the international debt crisis that emerged in the early 1980s. Lipsey (1999) argues that FDI has been the most dependable source of foreign investment for developing countries. Moreover, FDI is important in this sense not only because it entails the movement of financial capital but also because it is normally associated with the provision of technology as well as managerial, technical and marketing skills. But it has to be emphasized here that FDI does not necessarily involve the movement of financial capital, as the investor may try to raise funds by borrowing from financial institutions in the host country. Moreover, the other benefits of FDI may not materialize, or they may materialize at a very high cost for the host country.

Finally, FDI is thought to play a potentially vital role in the transformation of the former Communist countries. This is because FDI complements domestic saving and contributes to total investment in the (host) economy. It is also because FDI brings with it advanced technology, management skills and access to export markets. Again, these positive effects may not arise, or they may arise simultaneously with some adverse effects (Moosa, 2002).

## 1.3. FDI and MNCs

FDI may be classified into expansionary and defensive types. Chen and Ku (2000) suggest that expansionary FDI seeks to exploit firm-specific advantages in the host country. This type of FDI has the additional benefit of contributing to sales growth of the investing firm at home and abroad. On the other hand, they suggest that defensive FDI seeks cheap labor in the host country with the objective of reducing the cost of production. Chen and Yang (1999) suggested that a multinomial logit model can be used to identify the determinants of the two types of FDI in the case of Taiwan. Their empirical results indicated that expansionary FDI is influenced mainly by firm-specific advantages such as scale, R&D intensity, profitability and motives for technology acquisition. Defensive FDI, on the other hand, is shown to be influenced by cost reduction motives and the nexus of production networks. Both types of FDI are affected by the characteristics of the underlying industry.

Most FDI is carried out by multinational corporations (MNCs) which have become household names. Examples (without any particular order in mind) are Toyota, IBM, Phillips, Nestle, Sony, Royal Dutch Shell, IBM, GM, Coca-Cola, McDonald's, Daimler-Benz and Bayer. It is, however, difficult to pinpoint what constitutes an MNC, and there is not even an agreement on what to call these firms. The literature shows various "labels" for these firms, consisting of the words "international", "transnational", or "global" followed by any of the words "corporations", "companies" and "enterprises".

However, a distinction is made between the terms "international", "multinational" and "transnational". "The term 'multi-national firm' has evolved from changes in the nature of international business operations. The term "international business firm" referred traditionally to the cross-border activity of importing and exporting, where goods are produced in the domestic market and then exported abroad, and vice versa. The financial implications of these transactions pertain to the payment process between buyers and sellers across national frontiers. As international operations expand, the international firm may feel that it is desirable, if possible, to expand in such a way as to be closer to foreign consumers. Production will then be carried out both at home and abroad. Thus, a multinational firm carries out some of its production activity abroad by establishing a presence in foreign countries via subsidiaries, affiliates and joint ventures (these terms will be defined later). The financial implications become more significant. The foreign "arms" of a multinational firm normally have a different base or functional currency, which is the currency of the country where they are located. This setup results in a greater currency and financial risk in general. As cross-border activity expands even further, the distinction between "home" and "abroad" becomes blurred, and difficulties arise as to the identification of the "home country". What is created in this case is a "transnational firm". It remains the case that the relationship between multinationals and FDI is very simple: firms become multinational (or transnational) when they undertake FDI. Thus, FDI represents an internal organizational expansion by multinationals. In this book, we shall use the term "multinational corporation" (MNC) generally to imply the firms that indulge in FDI.

The link between FDI and MNCs is so close that the motivation for FDI may be used to distinguish between MNCs and other firms. Lall and Streeten (1977) distinguish among economic, organizational and motivational definitions of FDI. The economic definition places emphasis on size, geographical spread and the extent of foreign involvement of the firm. This definition allows us to distinguish between an MNC and (i) a large domestic firm that has little investment abroad; (ii) a small domestic firm that invests abroad; (iii) a large firm that invests in one or two foreign countries only; and (iv) a large portfolio investor that does not seek control over the investment.

UNCTAD, 1999 defines multinational corporations (which it calls transnational corporations) as "incorporated or unincorporated enterprises comprising parent enterprises and their foreign affiliates". A parent enterprise or firm is defined as "an enterprise that controls assets of other entities in countries other than its home country, usually by owning a certain equity capital stake". A foreign affiliate is defined as "an incorporated or unincorporated enterprise in which an investor, who is resident in another economy, owns a stake that permits a lasting interest in the management of that enterprise". Foreign affiliates may be subsidiaries, associates or branches. UNCTAD (1999) distinguishes between them as follows:

- A subsidiary is an incorporated enterprise in the host country in which another entity directly owns more than a half of the share-holders' voting power and has the right to appoint or remove a majority of the members of the administrative, management or supervisory body.
- An associate is an incorporated enterprise in the host country in which an investor owns a total of at least 10%, but not more than a half, of the shareholders' voting power.

- A branch is a wholly or jointly-owned unincorporated enterprise in the host country, which may take the form of a permanent office of the foreign investor or an unincorporated partnership or a joint venture. A branch may also refer to land, structures, immovable equipment and mobile equipment (such as oil drilling rigs and ships) operating in a country other than the investor's country.

Empirical studies of the behavior and characteristics of MNCs attempt to detect the characteristics that distinguish an MNC from purely domestic firms. The variables that have been found to be significant in the earlier literature are R&D expenditure, size of the firm, and foreign trade intensity, although other variables also appeared to be important. Vaupel (1971) obtained evidence showing that US MNCs (as compared with domestic firms): (i) incurred higher R&D as well as advertising expenditure; (ii) showed more net profit; (iii) had higher average sales; (iv) were more diversified; (v) paid higher wages in the USA; and (vi) recorded a higher export sales ratio. Vernon (1971) reached a similar conclusion using the same data set. Lall (1980), however, found that R&D, economies of scale and the possession of skill advantages favor exports more than foreign production (FDI) by US MNCs, whereas product differentiation promotes more foreign production than exports

FDI may take one of three forms: greenfield investment, cross-border mergers and acquisitions (M&As), and joint ventures. Greenfield investment occurs when the investing firm establishes new production, distribution or other facilities in the host country. This is normally welcomed by the host country because of the job-creating potential and value-added output. Sometimes, the term "brownfield investment" is used to describe a situation where investments that are formally an acquisition resemble greenfield investment. This happens when the foreign investor acquires a firm but replaces almost completely the plant and equipment, labor and the product line.

Foreign investment may increase host market productivity through improved resource allocation, increased competition, and expansion of local capabilities through a transfer of know-how. Expansion of local capabilities occurs if FDI introduces superior organizational practices, machinery and technologies and if know-how spills over to, and local rival firms. The scope for such spillovers depends on technological strength of the parent firm, the extent to which technologies are transferred to the affiliate, and the extent of integration of the foreign firm into the host market (OECD, 2007).

## 1.4. Research in FDI

Recently, India has experienced superlative economic growth for a developing country. In Chapter 3, we analyze Japanese subsidiaries in India. The success stories of East and South East Asian countries suggest that FDI is a powerful tool for export promotion since MNCs, through which most FDI is funneled, have well-established contacts and up-to-date information about foreign markets. However, the experience of other Asian countries cannot be automatically generalized to India, given the lower level of development of infrastructure and commodity markets (Srinivasan, 1998; Sharma, 2003). Our data concerns Japanese subsidiaries in India from 2001 through 2006 compiled in the Toyo Keizai database.

As with a foreign subsidiary, the establishment of a joint venture involves the transfer of capital from the home to the host country and must, therefore, be viewed as part of the overall phenomenon of foreign investment. Many host countries consider it important to limit joint ventures to minority participation, prohibiting foreign majority companies, in order to obtain greater operational control over foreign affiliates. It is, however, an open question whether dilution of foreign holding necessarily means reduction of foreign control. While host countries encourage joint ventures, certain preconditions and infrastructure improvements are essential for their growth (Sengupta, 1998). FDI flows consist largely of four categories of capital account transactions (commonly referred to as mode of entry), namely, greenfield investment (whereby an enterprise is created essentially from scratch); mergers and acquisition involving significant cross-border elements; earnings reinvested in foreign-owned companies; and cross-border loans and trade credits between related enterprises. The latter two are not of major concern in a development context, whereas reinvested earnings sometimes make up a significant part of FDI flows between mature economies.

Trends in the mode of entry of firms investing in developing countries differ considerably from those of developed countries, where greenfield investment continue to dominate. However, driven by privatization, merger and acquisition have become an increasingly important mode of entry in developing countries as well in recent years.

Chapter 4 explores the main determinants of the factors influencing performance of foreign investment in Japan as a developed country, based on an integrative perspective incorporating contingencies at both parent and subsidiary levels.

As the world's second largest national economy, Japan has long been a highly attractive market for the investors of business and industrial products. However, while many foreign firms maintain a significant presence in Japan, the performance of many others is often disappointing. The failure of foreign investors, including a great number of US firms, in the domestic Japanese marketplace has been attributed to several causes, including demanding and skeptical Japanese buyers, cultural differences, and even discrimination against non-Japanese products (Melville, 1999).

Drawing on data from a sample of 3500 Japanese affiliates of foreign firms, this study makes a number of contributions to the literature on foreign ownership and MNC performance. First, it builds upon prior research by given a comprehensive account of the various variables affecting performance, which are critical to understanding subsidiary performance. Second, our research extends existing literature by integrating parent firm factors with subsidiary factors. Third, we use several variables to assess the performance, covering different measures of firm performance such as net profit, return on sales (ROS) and return on assets (ROA). Fourth, we compare different aspects of ownership advantages including management and employee levels of foreign investment including the interactions between parent companies and subsidiaries. Fifth, we employed variables like manager authority, foreign manager, new graduate and foreign employees as proxies of knowledge transfer and development. Researchers have focused on the firm, industry, and country levels of explanatory variables for both home and host country. A review of the equity ownership literature indicates a preponderance of studies focusing on firm characteristics and host country characteristics.

Knowledge and technology transfer via four interrelated channels: vertical linkage with suppliers or purchasers in the host markets; horizontal linkages with competing or complementary companies in the same industry; migration of skilled labor; and the internationalization of research and development. MNCs generally are found to provide technical assistance, training and other information to raise the quality of the suppliers' products. Many MNCs assist local suppliers in purchasing raw materials and intermediate goods and in modernizing or upgrading production facilities.

Chapter 5 of this empirical study explores first the relationship between type of industry and firm's factors including ownership, experience, import and export ratio and MNCs' factors. Second, we examined the impact of country of origin, foreign ownership and parent's and subsidiary's factors on the asset growth ratio. The magnitude of foreign investment flows continued to set records through the last decade. In 2000, world total inflows reached 1.3 trillion US dollars or four times the levels of 5 years earlier. More than 80% of recipients of these inflows, and more than 90% of the initiators of outflows, were located in developing countries (OECD, 2002).

Building upon previous research, the present study investigates firm specific factors versus industry structure, and their effect on performance. However, a decidedly different approach is taken. First, we employed type of industry as dependent variable in order to examine the relationship of firm's factors with type of industry. Second, there are very few papers that used asset growth for performance appraisals. Third, we build hypotheses to test key aspects of the firm's factor theories in the stream. Fourth, parent's firm factors and subsidiary factors are operationalized and measured to determine the firm-specific factors' effect on asset growth ratio. Lastly, manufacturing firms are compared to service firms, which, surprisingly, has rarely been done.

Foreign investment influences growth by raising total factor productivity and more generally, the efficiency of resource use in the recipient economy. This works through three channels: the linkages between FDI and foreign trade flows, the spillovers and other externalities *vis-à-vis* the host country business sector, and the direct impact on structural factors in the host market.

The major impact of foreign investment on human capital in developing countries appears to be indirect, occurring not principally through the efforts of MNCs, but rather from government policies seeking to attract

FDI via enhanced human capital. Once individuals are employed by MNCs' subsidiaries, their human capital may be enhanced further through training and on-the-job leading. Those subsidiaries may also have a positive influence on human capital enhancement in other companies, with which they develop links, including suppliers (OECD, 2002).

Policy makers in some emerging markets — especially in those that are comparatively less developed and only loosely integrated into international trade systems — tend to see foreign investment as a possible vehicle for raising exports. The prevailing reasoning is that MNCs may increase the export orientation of domestic market through channels that include: their higher degree of sophistication in product quality, brand recognition and access to world markets; their potential for alleviating constraints on the use of the host market's factor endowment; and their longer-term impact on the international competitiveness of the host economy's business sector.

# Chapter 2

# A Review of Theories of Multinational Enterprises

## 2.1. Introduction

Until the 1960s, foreign direct investment (FDI) by companies was mainly seen as movement of international capital and explained by investment theories and portfolio considerations. The main argument for international investment was that it occurs due to different rates of return between countries. This view has obvious deficiencies: It does not correctly explain the empirically observable patterns of direct investment, e.g. the two-way direct investment flows between some major countries; it does not explain why companies from the same country and even within the same industry differed in their internationalization behavior and it does not consider differences between the motives for international purchase of a few foreign stocks bonds (i.e. portfolio investments) and for substantial equity ownership by domestic companies in foreign companies (i.e. FDI).

During the 1960s, the perception of the multinational firm changed and the first theory of the international firm was developed. This was the work of Steven Hymer, who undertook the development of a more comprehensive theory on FDI and MNCs, emphasizing the control companies get over foreign activities by means of FDI (see Forsgren, 2008, pp. 15–29, for a detailed description of Hymer's contribution). He argued that under perfect competition, all companies would have access to similar resources and technology. Since in this case local firms in a foreign market would have knowledge advantages, little FDI would occur because incumbents would have a competitive advantage over new entrants.

## 2.2. The industrial organization theory

Hymer (1976) developed the industrial organization hypothesis, which was extended by Kindleberger (1969), Caves (1982) and Dunning (1988). According to this theory, when a firm establishes a subsidiary in another country it faces several disadvantages in competing with local firms. These disadvantages emanate from differences in language, culture, the legal system and other inter-country differences. For example, MNCs may have to pay higher wages in the host country than do local firms, because employment with them is regarded by local workers as being more risky. If, in spite of these disadvantages, the firm engages in FDI, it must have some advantages arising from intangible assets such as a well-known brand name, patent-protected technology, managerial skills, and other firm-specific factors (Morschett *et al.*, 2015). According to Kindleberger (1969), the comparative advantage has to be firm specific, it must be transferable to foreign subsidiaries, and it should be large enough to overcome these disadvantages.

FDI may arise because it is difficult to sell or lease these intangible assets. Lall and Streeten (1977) argue that the matter is just not one of the preferences of the MNC, since many of the advantages or the intangible assets cannot be sold to other firms, either because they are inherent in the organization or because they are difficult or impossible to define, value and transfer. Intangible assets that cannot be sold, even though the MNC may want to do so, include the MNC's managerial and organizational capabilities, the experience and the spirit of its executives, its standing in financial markets, and its contacts with various officials and other firms.

"It is these firm-specific advantages that explain why a firm can compete successfully in a foreign market" (Moosa, 2002). This approach has been used by Graham and Krugman (1991) to explain the growth of FDI in the USA. One problem with this approach, however, is that it fails to explain why the firm does not utilize its advantages by producing in the home country and exporting abroad, which is an alternative to FDI.

According to Kindleberger, firms will be inclined to indulge in FDI in preference to exports if they operate with minimum costs at home, in which case additional production for exports would move them into a segment of rising costs. Moreover, lower production costs abroad may be achieved because of the procurement of cheap raw materials, an efficient transportation network, superior managerial skills, non-marketable technology and substantial investment in R&D in the home country.

Aharoni (1966) suggested another answer to this question based on the behavioral theory of the firm suggested by Cyert and March (1963). He argued that the three factors affecting the initial investment decision are uncertainty, information and commitment. Uncertainty is normally exaggerated, in which case some initial force (such as the fear of losing a market) propels the desire to indulge in FDI. This leads to a search for information relevant to project appraisal. Once business executives spend time and effort on the project, and if it is promising, then they will be committed to its implementation (Moosa, 2002).

## 2.3. The internalization theory

According to the internalization theory, FDI arises from efforts by firms to replace market transactions with internal transactions. This idea is an extension of the original argument put forward by Coase (1937) that certain marketing costs can be saved by forming a firm. For example, if there are problems associated with buying oil products on the market, a firm may decide to buy a foreign refinery. These problems arise from imperfections and failure of markets for intermediate goods, including human capital, knowledge, marketing and management expertise. The advantages of internalization are the avoidance of time lags, bargaining and buyer uncertainty. Indeed, the main motive for internalization is the presence of externalities in the goods and factors markets (Moosa, 2002). Buckley and Casson (1976) argue that if markets in intermediate products are imperfect, firms have an incentive to bypass them by creating internal markets, such that the activities linked by the markets are brought under common ownership and control. The internalization of markets across national boundaries leads to FDI, and this process continues until the marginal benefits and marginal costs are equal.

"The internalization theory explains why firms use FDI in preference to exporting and importing from foreign countries. It also explains why they may shy away from licensing. Because of the significant time lags and transaction costs associated with market purchases and sales, firms replace some of the market functions with internal processes; that is, with intra-firm transactions. Moreover, the internalization process eliminates uncertainty" (Moosa, 2002).

It is sometimes claimed that the internalization theory represents a general theory of FDI, whereas other theories are subsets of the general theory of internalization. Petrochilos (1989) argues that, while it is clear that MNCs do bypass the market for intermediate products through FDI, it is not certain that the motive for internalization is the external market's inefficiency in terms of high transaction costs and longer time lags, or anything else. He further suggests that a stronger argument is the one put forward by Dunning (1977), that firms want to retain the exclusive right of using the innovations generated by their R&D efforts. Buckley and Casson (2000) present what they call a formal extension of the internalization hypothesis by providing a model that attempts to explain variations in entry mode.

## 2.4. The location theory

FDI exists due to the lack of international mobility of some factors of production, such as labor and natural resources. This immobility leads to location-related differences in the cost of factors of production. However, locational advantage of low wages is the one form of location-related differences in the costs of factors of production. Thus, the level of wages in the host country relative to wages in the home country is an important determinant of FDI. "That is why countries such as India attract labor-intensive production (for example, footwear and textiles) from high-wage countries. It is also, why MNCs wanting to establish production facilities in North America would choose Mexico in preference to Canada. Of course, high wages may be indicative of high quality of labor, in which case the relationship between low wages and FDI does not hold" (Moosa, 2002). For example, activities such as banking and finance, and R&D, are not relocated to countries where people working in these fields earn low wages. What matters in this case is the quality of labor (see Wheeler and Mody, 1990). It is important to bear in mind that differences in cross-country labor productivity can be so significant that consideration of wage rates alone is not a reliable variable. Petrochilos (1989) points out that cross-country differences in labor productivity can explain partially why the bulk of FDI goes to high-wage industrial countries. After all, an investor may choose to locate in Canada rather than in Mexico.

Evidence on the theory that cheap labor attracts FDI is mixed. Evidence from survey reports is weak, as, for example, in Forsyth (1972). However, the results of some of the time series and cross-sectional studies are favorable. For example, Riedel (1975) found relatively lower wage costs to be one of the major determinants of export-oriented FDI in Taiwan. Goldberg (1972), Saunders (1983), Schneider and Frey (1985), Culem (1988) and Moore (1993) found that a rise in the host country's wages (given wage rates in the source country) would discourage FDI flows.

However, the rise in wages necessarily causes a change in the relative prices of factors of production, leading to a shift to more capital-intensive methods, and therefore to more FDI. An alternative explanation is provided by Yang *et al.* (2000, p. 47) based on changes in productivity. They suggest that when markets are imperfect, it is possible that gains in productivity do not fully reflect on labor, in which case wages do not rise in tandem with productivity. Therefore, an increase in the wage rate may be accompanied by a fall in labor costs (that is, wages adjusted for changes in productivity). If a fall in labor costs attracts FDI flows, it would look as if FDI flows and wage rates are negatively correlated. Another factor that pertains to the labor market is labor disputes, which should have an adverse effect on FDI inflows. The adverse effect on FDI would depend on two characteristics of industrial disputes: incidence and severity (Morschett *et al.*, 2015).

Of course, a related factor would be the extent of unionization in the host country. It is now conventional wisdom that MNCs prefer flexible non-unionized labor markets and, when unionization is present, decentralized firm-level wage bargaining processes over centralized ones. The underlying idea is that unionization leads to higher labor costs. In fact, it is this very idea that is used as the basis for endorsing legislation aimed at limiting the power of unions, and deregulating the bargaining power in highly-unionized industrial countries.

Locational advantages not only take the form of low wages; they are also applicable to other factors of production. For example, a firm may indulge in FDI by building a factory in a country where it is cheap to generate hydroelectric power. Similarly, a factory could be located near a copper mine in the host country if copper is an important input in the production process. This is a locational advantage because significant savings can be made on the cost of shipping copper from where it is produced to where it is used. Apart from these savings, the firm can avoid delays in the delivery of copper shipments arising from the time it takes to ship the metal and the red tape that may be involved in this operation. In general, the location hypothesis emphasizes the importance of unavoidable government constraints, such as trade barriers.

## 2.5.  The eclectic theory (OLI paradigm)

The eclectic theory was developed by Dunning (1977, 1979, 1988) by integrating the industrial organization hypothesis, the internalization hypothesis and the location hypothesis without being too precise about how they interrelate. "The eclectic theory aims at answering the following questions. First, if there is demand for a particular commodity in a particular country, why is it not met by a local firm producing in the same country, or by a foreign firm exporting from another country? And, second, suppose that a firm wants to expand its scale of operations, why does it not do so via other channels? These other channels include the following: (i) producing in the home country and exporting to the foreign country; (ii) expanding into a new line of business within the home country; (iii) indulging in portfolio investment in the foreign country; and (iv) licensing its technology to foreign firms that carry out the production. It seems that the answer to these questions is that a foreign subsidiary can out-compete other potential suppliers in the foreign market, and that FDI is more profitable than other means of expansion. Another question arises: why is this the case? The eclectic theory attempts to answer this question and the related questions" (Morschett *et al.*, 2015).

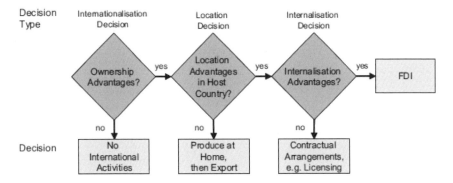

**Figure 2.1:**   The OLI decision process for foreign operation modes

*Source*: Sudarsanam (2003), Welch *et al.* (2007) and Morschett *et al.* (2015).

According to this theory, three conditions must be satisfied if a firm is to engage in FDI. First, it must have a comparative advantage over other firms arising from the ownership of some intangible assets. These are called ownership advantages, which include things like the right to a particular technology, monopoly power and size, access to raw materials and access to cheap finance. Second, it must be more beneficial for the firm to use these advantages rather than to sell or lease them. These are the internalization advantages that refer to the choice between accomplishing expansion within the firm or selling the rights to the means of expansion to other firms. Third, it must be more profitable to use these advantages in combination with at least some factor inputs located abroad. If this is not the case, then exports would do the job. These are the locational advantages, which pertain to the question of whether expansion is best accomplished at home or abroad (Figure 2.1).

Early research on FDI identified the role played by research and development. Large, research-intensive firms, typically resident in the most developed capital markets, were observed to dominate FDI (Vernon, 1966; Gruber *et al.*, 1967; Hirsch, 1967). The decision to undertake FDI was a stage in their growth strategy (Buckley & Casson, 1976). These firms were able to create differentiated products that could be competitive abroad (Vernon, 1966; Caves, 1971; Hymer, 1976). The ability for a firm to utilize its competitive advantage through foreign investment was said to depend on discovering product, locational or financial market imperfections that encourage FDI. Dunning (1958), Vernon (1966), Caves (1971), Hymer (1976), Buckley & Casson (1976), Dunning (1980) and Hennart (1989) pioneered the research establishing a comprehensive framework for explaining foreign investment. This became known as the OLI paradigm (ownership advantages, location advantages and internalization), and has been utilized intensively to the present time.

"The OLI paradigm proposes three questions about foreign investment: (1) based on present and potential ownership advantages, should a particular firm be involved in foreign markets? (2) Based on location advantages, where should the firm invest abroad? And (3) How should the firm serve foreign markets, should it be through internalization (FDI or sales subsidiaries) or through arms-length arrangements (such as licensing or export through intermediates)? The OLI paradigm offers a framework for answering these questions" (Moosa, 2002).

The "O" in the OLI paradigm relates to ownership-specific (firm-specific) advantages. In deciding whether to undertake FDI a firm must have developed firm-specific characteristics that enable it to be competitive in the home market. These characteristics must be transferable abroad and strong enough to compensate for the extra costs and barriers that confront those who try to do business abroad. Firm-specific characteristics typically possessed by successful MNCs are proprietary knowledge or know-how incorporated in: (1) economies of scale and scope; (2) managerial and marketing expertise; (3) advanced technology stemming from a heavy emphasis on research; and (4) differentiated products.

The "L" in the OLI paradigm stands for location-specific advantages that attract foreign investment to a particular market. The theory of internationalization and its corollary, network theory, attempt to answer the question of where to invest. Aharoni (1966) initiated the behavioral explanation of foreign investment, especially the initial decision of where to locate FDI. The behavioral approach has been extended by a formalized theory of the process of internationalization that explains not only the initial foreign investment decision but also the following reinvestment decisions. Network theory explains how the MNC and its subsidiaries interact and compete for power (Johanson & Vahlne, 1977;

Forsgren, 1989; Kogut & Zander, 1993; Chen & Chen, 1998; Pedersen & Petersen, 1998).

The current theory of internalization holds that it is critical for a firm to constantly upgrade proprietary information, and control the human capital that discovers and embodies it (Buckley & Casson, 1976; Krugman & Venables, 1994; Caves, 1996) . The "I" (internalization) factor in the OLI paradigm explains why a firm would choose to serve a foreign market through FDI rather than pursue alternative modes without ownership control of foreign activity.

The eclectic theory suggests that all forms of FDI can be explained by reference to its conditions. It recognizes that advantages arising from ownership, internalization and location may change over time, and accepts that if country-specific characteristics are important determinants of FDI, it may be invalid to generalize from one country's experience to another (Moosa, 2002).

## 2.6. The product life cycle theory

This theory is developed by Vernon (1966) to explain the expansion of US MNCs after the World War II. According to this theory, "products go through a cycle of initiation, exponential growth, slowdown and decline — a sequence that corresponds to the process of introduction, spread, maturation and senescence" (Vernon, 1971). Petrochilos (1989) points out that this hypothesis is useful because it offers another interpretation of FDI, particularly for manufactured products that are characterized by advanced technology and high-income elasticity of demand.

The product life cycle theory suggests that new products are likely to be discovered and initially produced in an industrialized market (e.g. US) due to the unique characteristics of the market. Subsequently, other industrialized markets (such as Europe and Japan) will be served by export, and then be followed by production in these industrialized nations. The production location would ultimately move, via European industrialized countries, to less developed countries (LDCs) with lower labor and/or production costs, and the US will import from these countries. It is plausible that, as the export market to the US grows and trade protectionism increases, foreign multinationals of newly industrialized countries (e.g. Korea or Taiwan) may invest in the US market, even if labor cost are generally higher in the US than LDCs.

This theory assumes that firms indulge in FDI at a particular stage in the life cycle of the products that they initially produced as innovations. The following main stages have been identified: in the first stage, the initial production takes place at home, close to the customers and because of the need for efficient coordination between R&D and production units. During this stage of the product life cycle, the demand for the new product is price inelastic, and so the innovating firm can charge a relatively high price. As time passes, the product is improved, based on feedback from customers. Up to this point, demand has come from customers living in the home country.

The second stage is marked by the maturity and export of the product to countries having the next highest level of income as demand emerges in these developed countries. As this demand continues to grow and competition emerges, the innovative firm resorts to FDI in these countries to meet local demand. At this stage, the home country is a net exporter of the product, while foreign countries are net importers.

The third stage is characterized by a complete standardization of the product and its production process, which is no longer an exclusive possession of the innovating firm. At this stage, price competition from other producers forces the innovating firm to invest in developing countries, seeking cost advantages. The home country starts to import the product from both domestic and foreign firms based in foreign countries. The home country becomes a net importer, while foreign countries are net exporters (Morschett *et al.*, 2015).

Hence, FDI takes place as the cost of production becomes an important consideration, which is the case when the product reaches maturity and standardization. FDI is thus a defensive move to maintain the firm-specific competitive position against its domestic and foreign rivals.

The product life cycle theory predicts that, over time, the home country where the innovative product first appeared switches from an exporting to an importing country. This prediction is consistent with the pattern of dynamic changes observed for many products. Agarwal (1980) describes a number of studies that support this theory. Gruber *et al.*

(1967) found a strong association between the propensity to invent new products, export performance, FDI, and the ratio of local production to exports on the one hand, and R&D expenditure of the US industries on the other. The association between the ratio of local production to exports and R&D expenditure is interpreted as an indication of the substitution of FDI for exports in host countries in the final stage of a product cycle.

## 2.7. The internal financing hypothesis

This hypothesis refers to the utilization of profit generated by a subsidiary to finance the expansion of FDI by an MNC in the country where the subsidiary operates. This hypothesis, which is based on the "gamblers' earnings" hypothesis of Barlow and Wender (1955), postulates that MNCs commit a modest amount of their resources to their initial direct investment, while subsequent expansions are financed by reinvesting profits obtained from operations in the host country. It therefore implies the existence of a positive relationship between internal cash flows and investment outlays, which is plausible because the cost of internal financing is lower. According to Froot and Stein (1991), one reason why external financing is more expensive than internal financing is informational imperfections in capital markets. The hypothesis seems to be more appropriate for explaining FDI in developing countries for (at least) two reasons: (i) the presence of restrictions on the movement of funds; and (ii) the rudimentary state and inefficiency of financial markets.

Hartman (1985) provides a tax-based explanation as to why MNCs like internal financing. He argues that, because repatriated earnings and not earnings of the subsidiary are typically the source of the tax liability in the home country, income tax should affect FDI differently, depending on the required transfers of funds from the subsidiary to the MNC. Hence, a firm should finance FDI out of foreign earnings to the greatest possible extent. That is, a firm's required foreign return is set at the point at which desired FDI just exhausts foreign earnings. As a result, Hartman draws a distinction between mature and immature foreign projects (or operations or subsidiaries), the latter being dependent on financing by the MNC without making any remittances.

## 2.8. The Kojima theory

Kojima (1973, 1975, 1985) views direct investment as providing a means of transferring capital, technology and managerial skills from the source country to the host country. This approach is described as being a "macroeconomic approach" or a "factor endowment approach", as opposed to the "international business approach" to FDI. Kojima classifies FDI into two kinds. The first is trade-oriented, which generates an excess demand for imports and an excess supply of exports at the original terms of trade. This kind of FDI leads to welfare improvement in both countries. Moreover, it would normally imply investment in industries in which the source county has a comparative disadvantage. This would promote trade and a beneficial industrial restructuring in both countries. The second kind is the anti-trade-oriented FDI, which has exactly opposite effects to those of the first kind. Thus, anti-trade-oriented FDI has an adverse effect on trade, and it also promotes unfavorable restructuring in both countries (Morschett *et al.*, 2015). Kojima argues that Japanese FDI has been trade-oriented, but not so the FDI of the USA. Thus, Kojima's hypothesis is based on the complementarity of trade and FDI, and it emphasizes the need for considering comparative costs.

## 2.9. Theories of entry modes

Theories of FDI deal implicitly with the mode of entry into foreign markets. In the 1960s, theories of FDI concentrated on the choice between exports and FDI. In the 1970s, the internalization hypothesis identified other modes of entry into a foreign market, including licensing, franchising and "arm's- length" arrangements such as subcontracting (Moosa, 2002). In the 1980s, M&As emerged as an important mode of entry, and so the choice became between acquisitions and greenfield FDI. Buckley and Casson (2000) distinguish between exporting, foreign licensing and FDI, as follows. Exporting is located domestically and controlled administratively; foreign licensing is foreign-located and controlled contractually; and FDI is foreign-located and controlled administratively. A number of studies have dealt with takeovers as a mode of entry, including Wilson (1980), Zejan (1990), and Agarwal and Ramaswami (1992). The theoretical issues have been surveyed by Svensson (1996) and Meyer (1998). Nitsch *et al.* (1996) relate entry mode to performance.

The issue of advantages of direct investment over exporting has been dealt with extensively in the literature. Lall and Streeten (1977) consider major factors that affect the choice between exports and FDI as follows:

- Production and transportation costs, as FDI enables them to exploit cost advantages.
- Government policy in the host country with respect to trade barriers.
- In general, firms tend to switch from exports to FDI when the destination countries start adopting import-substitution policies. We have seen that the threat of protectionism in the host country induces a shift from exporting to FDI (Blonigen and Feenstra, 1996).
- The marketing factor, as FDI enables firms to service the destination markets in a better way.
- Oligopolistic reaction in the sense that a move towards foreign production by one oligopolistic firm induces others to follow. This is indeed the oligopolistic reaction hypothesis presented earlier as a theory of FDI.
- Product cycle, which triggers FDI along the lines suggested by the product life cycle hypothesis.

Eaton and Tamura (1996) present a simple model of the choice between exports and FDI, showing that it depends on the host country's size, its level of technological sophistication, and the distance from the source country. They find that the importance of FDI relative to exports grows with population, and that distance tends to inhibit FDI much less than it inhibits exports. They also detect a tendency for Japanese exports to rise relative to FDI as countries become more advanced, and the opposite tendency for the USA.

Several factors identified to make FDI more attractive than licensing is defined by Lall and Streeten (1977) defined licensing as the sale of technology, brand names, patents, management services, or other similar assets. According to Baranson (1970), McManus (1972), Parker (1974) and Baumann (1975), FDI is preferred to licensing if: (i) the host country is politically stable; (ii) the technology is new and tightly controlled;

(iii) the firm is large and more internationally involved; (iv) the firm's sources of power are broadly based; and (v) the absorptive capacity of the licensee is low.

Conversely, licensing will be preferred over FDI if: (i) the technology is diffused widely; (ii) the host market is small and risky; (iii) the firm is inexperienced, risk averse or nationally-oriented; (iv) the advantage of the firm is specific; and (v) the potential licensee is big and capable. Of course, the decision does not have to be very black and white, and many intermediate positions are possible between investments in wholly-owned subsidiaries and licensing.

International joint ventures have also emerged as an important entry mode. Buckley and Casson (1988, 1996) summarize the conditions that are conducive to the establishment of joint ventures, including: (i) the possession of complementary assets; (ii) opportunities for collusion; and (iii) barriers to full integration. The literature has also focused on the selection of joint venture partners, management strategy, and performance measurement. Although MNCs prefer to have wholly-owned or majority-controlled subsidiaries, there are reasons why they would agree to take part in joint ventures. First, government policies in many developing countries make joint ventures the only available mode of entry. Second, the joint venture partners may provide complementary skills. Third, because joint ventures can be used as a means of alleviating country risk, particularly the risk of takeover. Joint ventures may also be attractive in cases where the project is too big for the MNC (Moosa, 2002).

Buckley and Casson (2000) present a model of market entry that has three distinctive features. First, it is based on a detailed schematic analysis that encompasses all of the major market entry modes. Second, it distinguishes between production and distribution. Third, the model takes account of the strategic interaction between the entrant and its leading host country rival after entry has taken place. They reach the following two conclusions: First, subcontracting is not a very attractive mode of entry, because it does not give access to the local rival's experience. Second, joint ventures in production do not make much sense as an entry mode unless the production joint venture is part of an integrated joint venture that handles distribution as well. Furthermore, if FDI is the chosen entry mode, another decision need to be made: whether FDI takes the form of greenfield FDI (the establishment of new production facilities), or mergers and acquisitions (M&As).

## 2.10. The classical theory of corporate governance

The observations of the paradoxes of power and control at the level of the modern corporation originate with Berle & Means (1965) and their work on the consequences of the separation of ownership and control. Fligstein & Freeland (1995) explored three internal control problems, and an even wider range of external control issues that extend the debate beyond the unbundling of ownership and control, from the literature. They argue that the corporation may encounter tensions and conflicts of interests in each of these relationships:

(1)   the control relationship between management and workers,
(2)   relationship between management and shareholders,
(3)   division of labor and the subsequent division of power and responsibilities within the corporation or intra-corporate intra-management relationships,
(4)   relationship with investors and capital markets,
(5)   relationships with suppliers,
(6)   relationships with competitors,
(7)   relationships with the state, with governments and other public institutions.

One may only speculate how each of these relationships could act as an important contributor to the increase or decrease of corporate productivity and performance. Therefore, the problems associated with investors' control that derive from the unbundling of ownership and control (Blair, 1995; Castanias & Helfat, 2001; Gupta *et al.*, 2002); is much more about the redistribution of rents among shareholders and residual claimants, rather than about improving corporate performance, or enhancing corporate capabilities, and capturing the value added by different corporate agents.

## 2.11. Agency theory

Agency theory deals with delegation relationships in which a principal delegates certain tasks and decisions to an agent based on an explicit or implicit contract. The actions taken by the agent influence the welfare of the principal. Contracts between the principal and the agent are always incomplete due to limited information, unpredictability of future situations and the high cost of complete contracts (Morschett *et al.*, 2015). Furthermore, the agent theory asserts that usually there is information asymmetry in favor of the agent. Before closing a contract, the principal is not able to identify fully the capabilities and characteristics of the potential agent (hidden characteristics) and this might lead to an adverse selection (Richter & Furubotn, 2003). More relevant for the case of MNCs, after the contract has been closed, the principal cannot completely observe the behavior of his agent (hidden action) and the result of the delegation is also influenced by external conditions that the principal also cannot fully observe (hidden information) (Elschen 1991; Woratschek & Roth, 2005). All this leaves room for opportunistic behavior on the part of the agent.

"Agency theory assumes that the agent intends to maximize his individual utility and that the objectives (and the risk preferences) of principal and agent may diverge. Thus, conflicts of interest may emerge. With the assumption of moral hazard, it is assumed that the agent will even carry out actions that influence the welfare of the principal negatively if it enhances his own benefit" (Morschett *et al.*, 2015).

Transferring this consideration to the headquarter-subsidiary relationship, the HQ cannot make all decisions itself since it does not have the necessary information and resources. When delegating decisions and actions to the foreign subsidiary, however, the interests of the subsidiary might diverge from its HQ. The agent theory attempts to suggest mechanisms for information, incentive and control that align the interests of the subsidiary with those of HQ (i.e. mechanisms that motivate the subsidiary to contribute to the overall objectives of the MNC) (Nohria & Ghoshal, 1994).

## 2.12. Transaction cost theory

Ronald Coase (1932) developed the transaction cost theory in a paper titled "The Nature of the Firm". He asserts that when a company tries to determine whether to outsource or to produce goods or services on its own, market prices are not the sole factor. There are also other factors such as transaction costs, search costs, contracting costs and coordination costs, in which determine whether a company uses internal or external resources for products or services.

Over the last decades, the dominant theories to explain internationalization and related concepts, e.g. the choice of foreign operation mode, have been the transaction cost approach (TCA) (Williamson, 1985) and the closely related internalization theory (Buckley & Casson 1976). This theory argue that companies internationalize in a way that minimizes the cost of cross-border transactions. Further, they consider the fact that it may be more efficient to internalize markets across borders. For example, a joint coordination of different activities in different countries may incur less transaction costs than using market mechanisms between countries.

Transaction costs refer to (i) search and information costs, i.e. costs incurred in determining that the required good is available on the market, who has the lowest price, etc.; (ii) bargaining costs, i.e. costs required to come to an acceptable agreement with the other party to the transaction, drawing up an appropriate contract, etc.; and (iii) monitoring and enforcement costs to ensure the other party sticks to the terms of the contract, and taking appropriate action if they do not. For example, monitoring costs might include measuring output (e.g. quality control in the factory of a supplier). If conditions change, contracts might have to be adjusted which incurs adjustment costs.

According to Morschett *et al.* (2015) the two basic assumptions of the TCA are:

- Bounded rationality, i.e. actors intend to act rationally but are only capable of doing so in a limited way, partly because they have incomplete information and partly because they have limited processing capacity.
- Opportunistic behavior, i.e. business partners are expected to use the incompleteness of contracts and changing circumstances for their own self-interest and only adhere to the contract if they are monitored.

The transaction cost theory is the most popular theory in explaining international mode choice decisions (Hennart & Park, 1993). Transaction costs are composed of the costs of finding and negotiating with an appropriate partner, and the costs of monitoring the performance of the partner. However, the essence of the transaction cost theory of FDI is to expand the cross border of business. This expansion is based on the ideas that locating facilities abroad are more efficient than exporting to the country from the parent company and that the company finds it desirable to invest in that foreign country (Hennart & Park, 1993). Research shows that transaction costs play a very important role in the finding of an efficient and successful market entry mode (Hennart & Park 1993). Furthermore, they have found that when transaction costs are low, firms tend to rely on the market to deliver required target market benefits e.g. joint venture subsidiary. As the costs increase, they tend to switch to more hierarchical modes such as wholly owned subsidiaries. The core dimensions of these transactions are the asset specificity, the frequency of economic exchange, and uncertainty surrounding the exchange of resources between the focal parties (Andersen, 1997).

To summarize, the TCA compares the costs of internalization of external markets with the costs of market transactions and cooperation (Figure 2.2). Under certain circumstances, markets are imperfect, and companies are forced to internalize transactions to compensate.

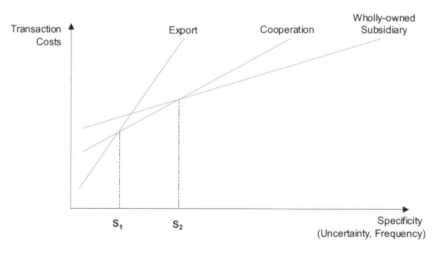

**Figure 2.2:**   Transaction cost reasoning for different modes of internationalization
*Source*: Welch *et al.* (2007) and Morschett *et al.* (2015).

The transaction cost theory has been criticized for the fact that psychic distance influence and institutional backgrounds are absent in the discussion of entry mode decisions (Morschett *et al.*, 2015). This is mainly due to the difficulties in understanding that social and cultural factors are only a part of the so-called transaction atmosphere and that interaction effects between socio-cultural and transaction costs factors cannot be determined in this simplified model theory (Schaefer, 2002). It has also been criticized for being unable to explain the evolution of entry modes (Lu, 2002) because it just offers a static view of organizational activities characterized by the absence of adequate social bonds.

## 2.13.  Resource-based theory

While the transactions cost theory focuses on transactions and analyses whether these are better carried out within the firm or between firms, the resource-based view (RBV) considers the firm as a bundle of resources (e.g. Wernerfelt, 1984; Barney, 1991).

Previous approaches (e.g. the industrial organization approach) assumed that firms within an industry are generally similar in terms of strategically relevant resources and that any heterogeneity that may develop is short-lived because resources are highly mobile or even tradable. Instead, the RBV assumes (Barney, 1991):

- Firms within an industry may be heterogeneous with respect to the strategic resources they control.
- Resources may not be perfectly mobile across firms.
- Therefore, heterogeneity may be long lasting.

Resources are broadly defined as "those tangible and intangible assets which are tied semi-permanently to the firm" (Wernerfelt, 1984) or, more precisely, as "all assets, capabilities, organizational processes, firm attributes, information, knowledge, etc., controlled by a firm that enable the firm to conceive of and implement strategies that improve its efficiency and effectiveness" (Barney, 1991). The resources categorize into physical capital resources (such as technology, geographic location, access to raw materials), human capital resources (employee experience, judgment, intelligence and insight) and organizational capital resources (formal structures, informal relationships among groups within a firm, coordinating systems, etc.). To be the basis for a sustained competitive advantage, resources have to fulfil a number of criteria (Dierickx & Cool, 1989; Barney, 1991) include:

- be valuable.
- be rare,
- be imperfectly imitable (and they must be imperfectly or not tradable),
- be no strategically equivalent substitutes that are valuable but not rare or not imperfectly imitable.

The RBV argues that firms possess resources, a subset of which enables them to achieve competitive advantage, and a subset of those that lead to superior long-term performance. Rare resources can lead to the creation of competitive advantage. This advantage can be maintained over long periods so that the company is able to protect the imitation, transfer or substitution of resources. The resource-based theory emphasizes factors internal to the firm. It argue that acquisition and retention of resources that are rare, non-substitutable and, in combination, difficult to imitate are a source of economic rent and accounts for the heterogeneity of firms' performance in any industry (Reed & DeFillipi, 1990; Mahoney & Pandian, 1992; Oliver, 1997).

According to this view, a company's competitive advantage derives from its ability to assemble and exploit an appropriate combination of resources. Sustainable competitive advantage is achieved by continuously developing existing resources and creating new ones and capabilities in response to rapidly changing market conditions. According to resource-based theorists like Grant (1991) and Peteraf (1993), firms can achieve sustainable competitive advantage from resources like strategic plans, management skills, tacit knowledge, capital, employment of skilled personnel among others. The assets and resources owned by companies may explain the differences in performance. Resources may be tangible or intangible and are harnessed into strengths and weaknesses by companies and in so doing lead to competitive advantage (Saffu & Manu, 2004).

## 2.14. Stages models of internationalization

The stages models of internationalization are rooted in the behavioral theory of the firm. These models (which the internationalization process model or Uppsala model) by Johanson and Vahlne (1977) propose a relationship between the knowledge of the decision makers in the company and the level of resource commitment in a foreign market.

The main assumption of this model is that companies with low market knowledge about a particular foreign market would prefer a low commitment to this market. When the company collects experimental knowledge in the market, it tends to commit additional resources. In the so-called establishment chain, the model proposes that foreign operation modes in a specific foreign country are switched along a certain path (Morschett *et al.*, 2015):

- No international activities.
- Export activities via agents.
- Export activities via the company's own sales subsidiaries.
- Establishment of production subsidiaries in the foreign country.

Furthermore, the Uppsala model suggests that companies often select foreign markets based on the psychic distance to that market and that internationalization often occurs along a psychic distance chain. Therefore, the common assumptions of all stages models are (Swoboda, 2002; Morschett *et al.*, 2015):

- Internationalization is a slow and gradual process.
- The process of internationalization is not the result of long-term strategic planning, but of incremental decisions.
- Internationalization is an adaptive process, and with time, resource commitment in the foreign market and changes in the management of the foreign organizational unit will occur.
- Internationalization is a process occurring in stages, characterized by different rates of change and unsteady development.
- During internationalization, companies accumulate experiential knowledge, which facilitates foreign activities and further internationalization.

In general, the stages models outlining foreign operation modes mainly through a particular knowledge of a company, which perceives uncertainty and, therefore, determines the willingness of the company to invest in that country (Morschett *et al.*, 2015). The network perspective of the MNC acknowledges that foreign subsidiaries are and should be heterogeneous: to be truly effective, multinational corporations should be differentiated (Nohria & Ghoshal, 1997).

Heterogeneous characteristics of subsidiaries include, inter alia (Morschett, 2007):

- Value-added activities carried out by the subsidiary, extend from single activities (e.g. only sales) to full value chains.
- Dominant motives for the establishment of the country subsidiary, for example, resource seeking or market seeking.
- Available resources and capabilities of the subsidiary.
- Local conditions of the host country, e.g. political and economic situation.
- Degree of horizontal and vertical product and communication flows with other subsidiaries and the headquarters.
- Control and influence of the headquarters.
- National, regional or worldwide responsibility of the subsidiary.
- Age of the foreign subsidiary or time frame of belonging to the MNC (in the case of an acquisition).
- Size of the subsidiary (sales, employees, financial assets, etc.)
- Performance of the subsidiary.

## 2.15.  Monopolistic advantage theory

The monopolistic advantage theory of FDI (developed by Hymer, 1966 and Kindleberger, 1969) asserts that the multinational corporations possess a rent yielding asset (e.g. production know-how) which gives them an edge in competing with firms in their home market, as well as with indigenous firms abroad. According to this theory, the multinational corporations have superior technology or product differentiation which enables them to compete in markets across globe. Therefore, it is likely that they would operate in monopolistic industries at home and abroad. Caves

(1971) argues that monopolistic advantages, which are created by both advertising and R&D investments, characterize not just specific firms but rather firms within oligopolistic industries. In fact, Gruber *et al.* (1967), Caves (1974) and Mansfield *et al.* (1979) reported that FDI tends to be associated with R&D intensity at the industry level. Knickerbocker (1973) assert that the timing of MNCs' foreign direct investments are largely determined by their oligopolistic reaction to competitors' investments. In a similar context, Vernon (1974) and Graham (1978) showed evidence that reverse foreign direct investments (RFDI) are also the reactions of non-US-based MNCs to the FDI done by US-based MNCs. Flowers (1976) suggests that the timing of European and Canadian FDI in the US can be explained by oligopolistic reactions.

If this argument is valid, reverse RFDI is expected to be heavy in manufacturing industries focused on research and development and advertising, since these industries invest abroad more extensively than others (Table 2.1).

**Table 2.1:** Some of researches in FDI and entry mode

| Authors | Sample | Research Focus/Questions | Major Findings |
|---|---|---|---|
| Erramilli (1989) | 463 US companies in the service industry | How do service firms enter foreign markets? How does the entry behavior vary across different industries in the service sector? | Firms' foreign entry behavior characterized by diversity due to unique characteristics: intangibility, perishability, heterogeneity, and inseparability. Entry mode in the hard services is similar to the manufacturing sector. Soft-services firms are more restricted in their entry mode choice (i.e., contractual entry, licensing, or franchising, FDI). |
| Gomes-Casseres (1990) | 187 US firms | Investigation of ownership preferences adopting transaction cost and institutional variables simultaneously. | When government ownership restrictions deter firm entry, relatively large firms and those with high intra-system sales are deterred more than others |
| Erramilli (1992) | 175 US companies | What effects do external and internal environmental factors have on the service firm's decision to integrate or not integrate its international business operations in a given entry situation? | Service firms choose integration modes when foreign market size, unavailability of host-country associates, and the firm's policy on maintaining control over foreign operations all become more influential in its entry mode choice process. Service firm's ability and tendency to integrate decreases when host-country restrictions on foreign ownership, environmental risk, and internal resource constraints all increase in importance and influence in its entry mode choice process. |

| | | | |
|---|---|---|---|
| Erramilli and Rao (1993) | 463 US service firms | How do service firms choose between full-control and shared-control entry modes? | The relationship between asset specificity and entry mode choice is moderated by numerous factors that either raise the costs of integration or decreases the firm's ability to establish full-control modes. When costs are low or the ability to integrate is high, firms characterized by low asset specificity establish full-control modes. As costs increase, low-specificity firms will increasingly choose shared-control modes. |
| Erramilli and D'Souza (1993) | 141 US firms in the service industries | Investigates foreign market entry behavior of small service firms. | Differences in entry mode choice between small and larger firms are insignificant at lower level of capital intensity. Small firms seem to show greater preferences for similar markets when capital intensity is high. When capital intensity is high, small firms prefer FDI modes significantly less than larger firms. |
| Woodcock *et al.* (1994) | 321 Japanese firms entering the US market | Examination of the relationship between ownership entry modes and firm performance. | Different entry modes have different performance outcomes based upon their resource and organizational control demands. New ventures should outperform joint ventures, and joint ventures should outperform acquisitions. |
| Brouthers *et al.* 1996 | 125 US-based computer software firms | Investigation of the impact of ownership and locational advantages on the choice of entry modes. | As a firm's ownership advantages increase, so does firm's use of more integrated entry modes. As a firm's perception of locational advantages increases, so does its use of more integrated entry modes. |

*(Continued)*

**Table 2.1:**   (*Continued*)

| Authors | Sample | Research Focus/Questions | Major Findings |
|---|---|---|---|
| Reuber and Fischer (1997) | 49 software firms in Canada | Investigation of the influence of the management team's international experience on the internationalization behaviors of SMEs. | Internationally experienced management teams have a greater propensity to develop foreign strategic partners and to delay less in obtaining foreign sales after start-up, and that these behaviors are associated with a higher degree of internationalization. |
| Brouthers, *et al.* (1999) | 819 German and Dutch firm entering central and eastern Europe | Investigation of the relationship between Dunning's OLI variables, entry mode selection, and managerial satisfaction with firm performance. | Firms perceiving high ownership-specific, location-specific, and internalization advantages tended to prefer more integrated modes of entry, such as wholly owned subsidiaries and joint ventures. |
| Burgel and Murray (2000) | 398 UK firms | Determination of what modes of foreign market entry small technology-based start-ups chose and what the primary reasons for their elected choices were (intermediaries versus export). | The majority of firms choose countries in Western Europe for their first market entry. Young firms choose entry modes that were not resource intensive (preference for intermediaries). Management's international experience had a significant impact on the choice of entry mode. |
| Crick and Jones (2000) | UK Firms | Examination of SME overseas market expansion strategies of firms involved in technological innovation and among others studying the rationale for initial market selection and mode of market entry. | Policy makers should consider an integrated perspective in firms' internationalization by offering appropriate support mechanisms as managers consider and undertake modes of entry other than exporting. Key decision-makers, ownership, managerial knowhow, networking had an important influence on the nature and pace of internationalization. |

| | | | |
|---|---|---|---|
| Davis *et al.* (2000) | 1383 US firms | Examination of entry modes choice based on two sources of isomorphic pressures, host-country institutional environment, and internal institutional environment. | Firms using wholly owned entry modes demonstrated high levels of internal (parent) isomorphism; those using exporting, joint ventures, or licensing agreements demonstrated external isomorphism. Those using multiple or mixed entry mode demonstrated low levels of isomorphic pressures. |
| Zahra *et al.* (2000) | 1417 US firms across industries | Examination of the effects of international expansion, as measured by inter-national diversity and mode of market entry, on a firm's technological learning and the effects of this learning on the firm's financial performance. | Lower control modes of entry have a negative effect on speed. Knowledge integration increases the breadth and depth of the technological learning. Technological learning enhances a company's performance. |
| Delios and Beamish (2001) | 1124 Japanese firms | Comparison of institutional, transactional, and experience influences on ownership decisions. | Experience and institutional factors were the most important influences on the ownership position taken in the foreign investment, while transactional factors had a much less important and a more ambiguous role. |
| Shi *et al.* (2001) | 218 Hong Kong firms to invest in China | What factors influence small Hong Kong manufacturing firms' choice of investment entry modes into Mainland China? (Wholly owned subsidiary versus joint venture). | Strategic variables: SMEs following an export-oriented strategy prefer WOS to JV, while firms following a market-seeking strategy prefer JV. Effects of firm-specific variables are mixed: International experience does not seem to affect the selection of FDI entry mode, firms with no or little host-country experience prefer WOS to JV. Firms with a relationship in China prefer JV to WOS. |

*(Continued)*

**Table 2.1:**   *(Continued)*

| Authors | Sample | Research Focus/Questions | Major Findings |
|---|---|---|---|
| Erramilli *et al.* (2002) | 201 hotel industries in the United States | Explanation of a firm's choice of non-equity mode based on the organizational capabilities framework. | Develop a theoretical framework based on the "organizational capability" perspective to explain the choice between two non-equity modes — franchising and management-service contracts, while previous studies are based on the premise that foreign market entrants choose a mode — equity or non-equity — that offers them most control given their particular circumstances. |
| Nakos and Brouthers (2002) | 450 Greek firms | Determination if Dunning's OLI framework is applicable to SME entry mode selection. | Dunning's eclectic framework did a good job of predicting SME entry mode selection in CEE markets (85%). However, not all of the OLI factors appeared to be important for SMEs (Ownership: International experience was not significant predictor). |
| Yiu and Makino (2002) | 364 subsidiaries; 10 firms Japan | Investigation of the choice between a joint venture and a wholly owned subsidiary. | Multinational enterprises tend to conform to the regulative settings of the host-country environment, the normative pressures imposed by the local people, and the cognitive mindsets as bounded by counterparts' and multinational enterprises' own entry patterns when making foreign entry mode choices. |

| | | | |
|---|---|---|---|
| Brouthers and Nakos (2004) | Dutch and Greek firms | Application of TCE to SME entry mode choices — determination if SME transaction cost mode choices provide superior performance to other mode choices. | TCE did a good job of explaining SME mode choice and SMEs that used transaction cost-predicted mode choices performed significantly better than firms using other modes did. Mode performance and mode choice may be closely related. |
| Roberto (2004) | 1330 entries, Italy | Investigation of the choice between greenfield investment and acquisition-based on location determinants. | The location determinants strongly differ according to the foreign entry mode. Foreign acquisitions are affected not only by supply of acquisition candidates but also by the other location characteristics, such as the demand level, public infrastructure, stock of foreign firms, and unit labor costs. |
| Herrmann and Datta (2005) | 112 market in United States | Examination of the CEO characteristics' influences on entry mode decisions. | Relationships between TMT characteristics and international diversification are more dominant in better-performing than in lower-performing firms. |
| Rasheed (2005) | 123 publicly manufacturing SMEs in the United States | Examination on how performance outcomes vary between equity and non-equity entry modes depending on the effects of domestic and foreign environmental factors. | Firms will have a higher rate of international revenue growth using non-equity-based (exporting) foreign market entry modes in growing domestic environments. International revenue growth is higher for equity-based modes when foreign market risks are high. |

*(Continued)*

**Table 2.1:** *(Continued)*

| Authors | Sample | Research Focus/Questions | Major Findings |
| --- | --- | --- | --- |
| Meyer and Nguyen (2005) | 731 firms Vietnam | Investigation of how institutions in an emerging country influence market entry strategies. | The availability of scarce resources affects the location of FDI and the likelihood of greenfield entry. Institutional pressures arising from incumbent state-owned firms and the domestic market orientation of the investor lead to a preference for joint venture entry. |
| Somlev and Hoshino (2005) | 751 subsidiaries Japan | Examination of the effect of location factors on the establishment and ownership choice of MNEs. | Host competitiveness, host-culture type, and industrial growth are the most appropriate location predictors for entry mode. Location variables are important determinants of expansion strategy, indispensable in analyzing subsidiaries of MNEs even in hosts with stable political environment. |
| Blomstermo *et al.* (2006) | 140 Swedish service firms | Examination of the relationship between foreign market entry modes and hard and soft services. Which foreign market entry modes service firms opt for and if this influenced by systematic differences between types of service industries? | Soft-service firms are much more likely than hard-service firms to choose a high-control entry mode over a low-control entry mode. As cultural distance increases, the likelihood of this choice increases even more. |

| Author (Year) | Sample | Purpose | Findings |
|---|---|---|---|
| Ferna'ndez and Nieto (2006) | Sample of Spanish SMEs | Analysis of the relationship between the internationalization strategies of SMEs and types of ownership. | Internationalization is negatively related to family ownership and positively related to corporate ownership. The presence of a corporate block holder in family firms encourages internationalization. Ownership type influences the decision to internationalize. |
| Lu and Beamish (2006) | 164 Japanese SMEs | Examination of the effect of two internationalization strategies, exporting and FDI, on SME performance (ROA), the moderating influence of SME age at the time of its internationalization. | Exporting activity has a positive impact on growth, but a negative impact on profitability. FDI activity has a positive relationship with growth, but a U-curve relationship with profitability. An SME's age when it starts to make FDIs has a negative moderating impact on the relationship between FDI and firm growth and profitability. |
| Zain and Ng (2006) | Indigenous Malaysian small and medium-sized enterprises (SMEs) | How is the internationalization process of SMEs manifested in their choices of foreign markets and modes of entry? How do network relationships of SMEs impact their international market development? How do network relationships of SMEs impact their marketing-related activities within international markets? | Foreign market entry mode choice is facilitated by network contacts. Network relationships helped the software firms in encouraging them to engage in higher-commitment modes. |

*(Continued)*

**Table 2.1:** *(Continued)*

| Authors | Sample | Research Focus/Questions | Major Findings |
|---|---|---|---|
| Ojala and Tyrvainen (2006) | Eight software firms in Finland and Japan | Connection between a small software firm's business model (product strategy, revenue logic, distribution model, and service and implementation model) and the choice of entry mode. | Product strategy of software firms has a strong connection to the selected entry mode, while the use of a certain distribution model does not seem to be connected to the choice of entry mode. |
| Pinho (2007) | 600 potential Portuguese Companies | Do ownership-specific advantages impact on entry mode decisions? Do market-/location-specific advantages impact on entry mode decisions? To which extent do managerial and ownership dimensions impact on the choice of an equity entry mode? | The firm's international experience, its ability to innovate, the market potential for growth, and market-specific knowledge are key predictors for choosing an equity entry mode. SMEs are rather flexible in nature, minimizing the relevance of the perceived risk associated with the host country. |
| Li and Qian (2008) | A sample of 166 large, small, and medium-sized firms in technology industries | Comparison of large firms against SMEs in technology industries and assessment of the differences between them in the choices between partnership and self-reliance entry modes. | With violent market dynamism, entry mode choice of SMEs and MNEs differ (MNEs: self-reliance entry modes, SMEs: partnership entry modes). When high promotional effort is required, entry mode choice of SMEs and MNEs do not differ (partnership entry modes). |
| Cheng (2008) | Mail survey and secondary data collection. | Examination of the determinants of the choice of ownership-based entry mode strategy for SMEs in international markets. | Equity joint ventures may be the favored entry mode for less experienced SMEs to reduce cultural barriers. |

| | | | |
|---|---|---|---|
| Brouthers *et al.* (2008) | 160 Dutch and Greek firms in Central and Eastern European markets | To add a real option perspective providing a method for balancing the desire to minimize exposure to uncertainty while preserving an option to take advantage of upside benefits to predict a firm's mode choice. | Firms that used the combined real option/transaction cost-predicted choices had significantly higher levels of subsidiary performance satisfaction than firms that did not. |
| Ripolles Meliá *et al.* (2010) | 600 international service firms/ Spain | Examination of how innovation can help service SMEs to enter foreign markets more quickly and what the effects of a more rapid international involvement are? | Innovation orientation accelerates the firms' internationalization time; innovative firms opt for high-control entry modes in foreign markets. Two different models of internationalization within the services sector exist: firms either adopt a gradual process or attempt to benefit from a rapid transition period of internationalization. |
| Ghahroudi (2011) | 3500 foreign companies in Japan | Explores the impact of knowledge transfer and firm factors, parent firm specific, and subsidiary. Characteristics on foreign affiliated performance. | When a subsidiary operates in the manufacturing industry, MNCs prefer to have a majority of equity ownership. Foreign ownership ratio has a positive relationship with knowledge transfer factors, import, and export ratio of foreign affiliates. |
| Schwens *et al.* (2011) | 227 German SMEs | Examination of informal institutional distance and formal institutional risk as moderators on the relationship between frequently examined decision-making criteria and the entry mode decision of SMEs. | Major decision-making criteria of entry mode choice are contingent on the moderating effect of institutional context. |

*(Continued)*

**Table 2.1:** (*Continued*)

| Authors | Sample | Research Focus/Questions | Major Findings |
|---|---|---|---|
| Prashantham (2011) | Survey of 102 Indian software SMEs indicates | What enables some internationalizing SMEs to become micro-multinationals rather than pure exporter? | Higher stocks of cross-border social capital facilitate the adoption of higher-commitment entry modes. |
| Ripolle's *et al.* (2012) | 135 Spanish firms | Analysis of company-specific factors that can enhance the choice of higher-resource commitment entry modes in International New Ventures. | International market orientation as a key aspect in INV's choice of entry modes involving higher commitment of resources. Entrepreneurial orientation and early international entry act as antecedents to the development of an international market orientation. |
| Maekelburger *et al.* (2012) | 206 small and medium-sized enterprises in German | The relationship between asset specificity and foreign market entry mode choice in the context of SMEs by introducing knowledge safeguards (international experience, host-country networks, imitation) and institutional safeguards (property rights protection, cultural proximity). | Knowledge safeguards and institutional safeguards weaken the effect of asset specificity on the choice of equity foreign market entry modes. |
| Liu (2017) | The solar photovoltaic industry/32 in-depth interviews with entrepreneurs | Investigate the role of transnational entrepreneurs in growing born global firms, with a focus on the growth process facilitated by collaborative entry mode. | Initial public offering in overseas stock exchange accelerates the high growth trajectory of a born global firm by signaling its maturity. |

# Chapter 3

# Entry Strategies and Survival of MNC's Subsidiaries

## 3.1. Introduction

In recent years, the study of foreign direct investment (FDI) and related subjects (entry strategies, joint ventures, knowledge-transfer, cultural distance, parent and subsidiary performance, etc.) has attracted the attention of scholars from diverse fields such as economics, international business, organization theory and strategic management (Sinha, 2005). The literature has identified different factors that affect internalization, entry modes and subsidiary performance. However, few have used the survival of subsidiaries as a dimension of performance. In this study, we examine the subsidiary survival rate using information about subsidiaries available in the Toyo Keizai database. In addition, we analyzed the sales growth ratio as a measure of subsidiary performance to achieve a multidimensional understanding of the effect of entry strategies, subsidiary age, number of employees and equity ownership.

Recent theoretical work has increasingly modeled the positive effects of FDI on local entrepreneurship through backward and forward linkages, showing that foreign firms may foster the development of domestic firms in the host country (Markusen & Venables, 1999). Previous studies have been concentrated on subsidiary performance while operating in developed countries such as the US (Li & Guisinger, 1991;

Vega-Cespedes & Hoshino, 2002; Chung, 2001) and Europe (Nitsch *et al.*, 1995; Brouthers & Werner, 1999; Dörrenbächer & Gammelgaard, 2006). Scholars have also examined subsidiary performance when operating in developing countries such as China, Thailand, Latin America and Brazil (Luo, 1996; Makino & Beamish, 1998; Siripaisalpipat & Hoshino, 2000; Chen & Hu, 2002; Ogasavara & Hoshino, 2007a). However, few studies examine the impact of capital, subsidiary age, ownership and number of employees on the survival of subsidiaries. There are also few studies (see Chung, 2001; Chen & Ku, 2000; Pangarkar & Hendry, 2003) that used sales growth in order to measure subsidiary performance. We studied the effect of subsidiary age and number of employees (as a measure of subsidiary size), entry strategy and equity ownership on the sales growth ratio as a measure of performance.

In the ASEAN countries, the Andean Pact countries, and others including Bangladesh, Brazil, Kenya, Republic of Korea, Mexico, Nigeria and Pakistan, majority foreign ownership is explicitly permitted in priority, pioneer or promoted industries. Most countries also permit it in export-oriented companies. On the other hand, from 1973 to 1991, India limited foreign holdings generally to 40%, except in the export zones.

For the past two decades, India has experienced superlative economic growth for a developing country. There is hardly a facet of Indian psyche that the concept of "foreign" has not permeated. This term, connoting modernization, international brands and acquisitions by MNCs in popular imagination, has acquired renewed significance after the reforms initiated by the Indian government in 1991.

Until recently, India's local firms have been viewed only as passive recipients of technology, faced with the challenges of overcoming many disadvantages *vis-à-vis* MNCs. The predominant view of local firms and entrepreneurs, at least until recently, accepted a persistent status as low-cost, low-skill operations (Parthasarathy & Aoyama, 2006).

In this study, we analyze Japanese subsidiaries in India. The success stories of East and South East Asian countries suggest that FDI is a powerful tool for export promotion since multinational companies, through which most FDI is funneled, have well-established contacts and up-to-date information about foreign markets. However, the experience of other

Asian countries cannot be generalized to India, given the lower level of infrastructure and commodity markets (Srinivasan, 1998; Sharma, 2003). Our empirical setting is Japanese subsidiaries in India from 2001 to 2006 using the Toyo Keizai database.

## 3.2. Theoretical background and hypotheses

Since the mid-1980s, Japan has been one of the largest sources of FDI in the world. Japanese corporations actively pursue overseas investments in response to yen appreciation, protectionism, increasing labor costs, slower domestic growth and the need to secure natural resources and markets. Developing countries, such as India, are particularly vulnerable as they lack infrastructure such as communication, training, education, etc. India is required to maintain previous technology but is nevertheless eager to set up new industrial plants. As a result, localities compete globally to attract multinational companies for their investment and capital. In this process, they often ignore the safety and health violations that many MNCs engage in. Operations in developing countries confer a competitive advantage upon MNCs because they offer low-cost labor, access to markets and lower operating costs. Once there, companies have little incentive to minimize environmental and human risks.

FDI is a form of long-term international capital movement accompanied by investors' intangible assets, such as the stock of technological knowledge accumulated by R&D or the accumulation of marketing know-how from past advertising activity (Ito & Fukao, 2005). FDI includes significant investments by foreign affiliates, such as the construction of production facilities or ownership stakes taken in some countries. FDI not only creates new jobs, it can also lead to an infusion of innovative technologies, management strategies and workforce practices.

The purpose of FDI is to maintain long-term control of the management of the subsidiary. In addition, FDI is a means of accessing profit through purchase of equity in a foreign corporation. Contrary to the prevailing views that advocate an equal sharing of equity, performance was found to improve with increasingly unequal levels of ownership (Ramaswamy *et al.*, 1998). Japanese FDI in India was motivated by the desire to access local markets. It involved minimal transfer of technology and management skills. Japanese subsidiaries in India are operated independently (Anand & Delios, 1996).

Contrary to the grand narrative of 1991 based on the "opening of the flood-gates" idea, what took place in India was a gradual process of changes in policies on investment in certain sub-sections of the Indian economy. As a result of controversy surrounding FDI, owing to a lack of understanding, it has become the focus of a political storm (Singh, 2005).

Moreover, Japanese direct investment in Southeast Asia contrasts with FDI into the OECD countries[1] where it is mainly horizontal (i.e. it is done with the aim of serving local markets). For example, Yoshida (2004) finds approximately 90% of Japanese affiliate production in North America is sold locally in the US and Canada, while less than 1% of Japanese production in Europe is exported out of Europe. In contrast, the overwhelming majority of Japanese manufacturing affiliates in East Asia perform assembly and finishing operations, suggesting these affiliates serve in either a vertical FDI or export-platform capacity.

Lu & Hebert (2005) studied the moderating effects of asset specificity and uncertainty on the relationship between foreign parent equity control and international joint venture (IJV) survival in an empirical setting of Japanese IJVs in 12 Asian countries in the 1985–1996 periods. Their findings suggest that in the presence of high asset specificity, high levels of foreign equity control can lead to higher IJV survival rates. In addition, social knowledge can serve as a substitute for equity control in IJVs and contribute to higher IJV survival rates. Empirical evidence suggests that survival correlates positively with financial and satisfaction measures of performance (Geringer & Hebert, 1991). Post-entry survival of subsidiaries of multinational enterprises has received much attention from scholars. Previous studies reported that joint ventures have a very high failure rate (Kogut, 1989; Makino & Beamish, 1998). However, according to Hennart

---

[1] Organization for Economic Cooperation and Development (OECD). A multidisciplinary international body made up of 30 member countries that offer a structure/forum for governments to consult and co-operate with each other in order to develop and refine economic and social policy. While the OECD does not set rules and regulations to settle disputes like other international bodies, it encourages the negotiation of agreements and the promotion of legal codes in certain sectors. Its work helps the member countries to formalize both binding and non-binding agreements. The OECD is best known for its publications and statistics.

*et al.* (1998), past authors focused solely on joint ventures, implicitly counting exits by either divestiture or dissolution as "failures", leading to misinterpretation of statistical results. Investments involving small ownership levels also have very high mortality rates. Those with high ownership levels have mortality rates comparable to that of wholly-owned subsidiaries (Ogasavara & Hoshino, 2007a).

Based on previous research, we present our hypotheses as follows. Our first hypothesis considers whether MNCs have different entry strategies in different periods based on the year of establishment.

**H1.** *The probability of establishing a wholly-owned subsidiary is positively correlated with establishment year.*

The majority of Japanese FDI in recent periods has been in the form of wholly-owned subsidiaries (Beamish & Inkpen, 1998). The establishment of subsidiaries in developing countries has usually been theoretically related to taking advantage of the cheaper cost of resources, as well as a higher risk. Consequently, it is predicted that the subsidiaries frequently reveal features such as a large number of employees, low amounts of equity, manufacturing activities (rather than service activities) and a greater incidence of joint ventures. On the other hand, subsidiaries in developed countries are usually related to the sale of production and the delivery of services. They are usually wholly owned and require a higher level of investment.

While in some countries the domestic market is the target, in some Asian countries such as China and India, the government of the host country limits the level of foreign ownership in local companies. These countries have pushed MNCs to set up international JVs with local firms, rather than creating wholly ownership subsidiaries (WOS) as a means for local partners to acquire knowledge (Anand & Delios, 1996). However, the second hypothesis considers size.

**H2.** *The firm size of subsidiary measured by number of employees is negatively associated with subsidiary survival.*

Some scholars used the number of employees to measure the size of a company (Rasiah, 2003; Ogasavara & Hoshino, 2007a). The literature tells us that not only does the probability of survival increase with the size of a firm, but also the variable exerts a positive interactive effect on this probability. Key survival factors includes the pre-existence of relationships with firms, prior experience, the size of the entrant at start-up and the size of the parent (Tschoegl, 2000). Innovation has a positive and significant effect on the probability of a firm's survival. This effect increases over time and is conditional on the firms' age and size; the small and young firms are the most exposed to the risk of exit (Cefis & Marsili, 2006). The US industrial sector displays heterogeneity among firms on the basis of their size: smaller firms exhibit a higher profit rate, lower survival probability and difficulty in accessing the capital market (Dhawan, 2001). This suggests our third hypothesis.

**H3.** *Wholly-owned subsidiaries are more likely to survive than minority-owned subsidiaries.*

In the Lu & Hebert (2005) study, a high level of foreign equity control can lead to higher IJV survival rates. We expected that when a subsidiary has a greater equity ownership, especially full ownership, it is supposed to have more chance to survive. Wholly-owned offers firms the highest levels of control, since there is no problem of having to integrate different cultures, divergent strategic viewpoints and separate policies (Nitsch *et al.*, 1996). However, it requires the highest resource commitments, it is a high investment risk, and the firm has the disadvantage of being "foreign" in the local environment. This disadvantage stems from a lack of local knowledge which comprises information and know-how about the local economy, politics, culture and business customs of a region, information on local demands and tastes, as well as information on how to access the local labor force, distribution channels, infrastructure, raw materials and other factors required for the conduct of business in the host country (Makino & Delios, 1996). The fourth group of hypotheses considers effects on ownership mode.

**H4a.** *Manufacturing sector subsidiaries are more likely to be majority owned than service sector subsidiaries.*

Scholars have debated whether the determinants of foreign entry decisions are the same for service and manufacturing firms (Bouquet *et al.*, 2004).

We examine whether the industry differences of subsidiaries has an impact on equity ownership. When the subsidiary has been established as a manufacturing firm, MNCs prefer to have a greater equity of ownership.

**H4b.** *The age of a subsidiary is positively associated with the probability of establishing majority ownership.*

Previous findings suggest that Japanese MNCs increase their ownership level with time (Beamish & Inkpen, 1998; Mansour & Hoshino, 2002). We expected, in different periods of foreign investment, parent companies were interested in different entry rates or equity ownership. In recent periods, MNCs operate more subsidiaries with majority-owned equity than minority or co-owned subsidiaries.

The fifth set of hypotheses concerns effects on sales growth rate of subsidiaries.

**H5a.** *Older subsidiaries are likely to have a greater sales growth ratio than younger subsidiaries.*

International management capabilities can be learned from international experience with foreign markets in general, as well as prior experience with a specific country and experience from operating a particular foreign subsidiary (Ogasavara & Hoshino, 2007a). Given that subsidiaries with longer experience are considered to enjoy greater experiential and tacit knowledge, age is considered to provide a significant relationship with sales growth.

**H5b.** *Subsidiaries established as joint ventures are likely to have a greater sales growth ratio than wholly-owned subsidiaries.*

**H5c.** *Majority-owned subsidiaries are likely to have a greater sales growth ratio than minority-owned subsidiaries.*

WOS typically offer the benefits of whole profits and greater control over the operations of a foreign subsidiary. However, since a foreign affiliate is the sole owner, it must expend greater resources in establishing the operation. In a joint venture, considerable resources need to be spent in finding a partner. The risk of choosing an inappropriate partner is also borne by the MNC parent. Partners must also work together to integrate different corporate cultures, divergent strategic viewpoints and separate politics (Pan & Chi, 1999). Some studies argue that joint ventures are intrinsically inefficient because of the inherently complex management relationships (Makino & Beamish, 1998; Pangarkar & Hendry, 2003). The study of Ogasavara & Hoshino (2007a) proposed that entry mode selection not only has an impact on performance, but also that some industry and firm-specific advantages (ownership and internalization advantages) have an effect on subsidiary performance. Ownership and internalization advantages have both a positive and negative impact on performance. On the other hand, multinational experience showed a negative association with performance.

Without total ownership of its foreign subsidiaries the MNC would face higher transactional monitoring costs (or transaction cost) of its relationships with its subsidiaries. Ownership control through FDI is thus a response to market imperfections in the market for intermediates, such as knowledge, management and corporate control. One option for the MNC is to sell its expertise to foreign firms. However, the intermediate markets for such transfers are imperfect and would undervalue the potential value of the transfer. Therefore, an MNC would find it more profitable to exploit its ownership-specific advantages through FDI. In this manner, a larger value-added potential from the output of the firm's research could be retained in the MNC. The OLI paradigm does not explicitly address how finance-specific agency costs might affect FDI.

## 3.3. Research design and methodology

### 3.3.1. Sample and data collection

This empirical study examines the establishment, survival, size, entry strategy, equity ownership and sales growth of Japanese subsidiaries in India. The main data source used in this study is the Toyo Keizai databank (2001–2006) Japanese Overseas Investments (Kaigai Shinshutsu Kigyou Souran) listed by host country. The Toyo Keizai databank is an annual report that provides extensive information on the overseas activities of Japanese subsidiaries like the year of establishment, capital, employees, sales and ownership. We also used the Nikkei Annual Corporation Report 2005 (Nikkei Kaisha Nenkan: Jyoujyou Kaishaban) for additional information about Japanese companies.

The initial sample dataset contains a list of 270 Japanese subsidiaries in India, established by Japanese Multinational Companies from 2001 to 2006.

The unit of analysis of this study is the subsidiary sales based on financial data available between the years 2001 and 2006. From the initial sample of 270 subsidiaries, the sample was reduced to 263 cases for analyses of survival and majority ownership. However, due to incomplete data for sales and some of independent variables used in this study, we used a final count of 85 subsidiaries for the analysis of sales growth ratio as a proxy for the firm's performance.

## 3.3.2. Description and measurement of variables

### 3.3.2.1. *Dependent variables*

For this study, we used three dependent variables based on our hypotheses. The first dependent variable is subsidiary survival as a dummy variable, coded "zero" for closed or divested subsidiaries, and "one" for survivor subsidiaries. The second dependent variable is the majority-owned subsidiary as dummy variable, 1 if the equity ownership for subsidiary is equal or greater than 51% and 0 otherwise. The third dependent variable is the sales growth ratio, the measure of a firm's financial performance. Previous studies on Japanese MNCs have used the Toyo Keizai database as the main source of subsidiary performance (Delios & Beamish, 2001), measured by profitability on a scale of three performance levels (loss, break-even and gain). Some scholars used the return on sales (ROS), defined as profit before tax divided by total sales, and also return on equity (ROE) to gauge subsidiary performance (Geringer & Hebert, 1991; Ogasavara & Hoshino, 2007a). Performance data at the subsidiary level are frequently omitted from consolidated reports and consequently are very difficult to obtain. Therefore, the performance measure was derived from the Toyo Keizai database and represents only information the Japanese firms are willing to provide. Given Japanese firms' private nature, the information about sales is limited in this database. The sales growth ratio, defined as the average annual growth rate in total sales 2001–2006, is used as a measure of subsidiary performance.

### 3.3.2.2. Independent variables

This study adopts independent variables such as subsidiary age, entry strategy, majority owned, full ownership, subsidiary size and capital as well as industry dummies as the control variables.

The age of a subsidiary measured as the number of years that the subsidiary was operated (establishment year). The age of the subsidiary is important since it may relate to increasing independence (Hannon *et al.*, 1995).

In this empirical study, the entry strategy is based on the form of entry, including joint venture and wholly-owned subsidiary. Previous empirical researches on subsidiaries have found that wholly-owned subsidiaries outperform joint ventures. Entry mode selection is one of the most important decisions faced by MNCs that are expanding in nations outside their home locations, whereby WOS (Wholly-Owned Subsidiary) and joint venture entail direct investment in business sites in the target country.

A subsidiary is wholly-owned when the parent company has full ownership and full responsibility for controlling and managing the operations. On the other hand, a joint venture is a newly formed entity that involves a local and/or a foreign partner who share ownership, management, risks and rewards. The international business literature has defined a joint venture by the percentage of equity held by the foreign parent (Ogasavara & Hoshino, 2007a; Rasouli, 2011). A subsidiary with 95% or greater ownership is considered to be wholly owned, coded 0. However, a subsidiary with less than 95% ownership is a joint venture and is coded as 1 for entry strategy variable.

The number of employees is used as a measure of the firm size of subsidiary in logarithmic form. Since the distribution of the number of employees' values, as a proxy for subsidiary size, does not follow the normal distribution curve, the natural logarithm is applied to smooth the values and to bring them closer to normal distribution.

We divided the ownership based on the percentage of equity held by the MNC into three categories, majority-owned, co-owned and minority-owned subsidiaries. Majority owned is defined as a subsidiary with greater than 50% of equity ownership, co-owned when it is equal to 50% equity and minority owned when the subsidiary has less than 50% equity. We coded 1 if the subsidiary is majority owned, and 0 for other types of equity.

Full ownership measures as 100% equity ownership. We used full ownership as a dummy variable which, when the subsidiary has 100% ownership, is coded 1, and otherwise coded 0.

### 3.3.2.3. *Control variables*

A wide range of factors have an impact on a subsidiary's performance. By incorporating appropriate control variables, we can be assured that findings have been adjusted for other potential impacts (Pan & Chi, 1999). The performance level of firms in one industry may be different from other industries. To avoid biases, as in Brouthers *et al.* (2002), we included a dummy variable to control industry effects on the sales growth ratio, a value of 1 for manufacturing firms and 0 for service firms. We also employed the type of industry as an independent variable in order to analyze its effect on majority-owned subsidiaries. In this study, we used capital as an independent variable in order to see the effect on subsidiary survival, majority-owned subsidiaries and also as a control variable for sales growth ratio regression models. We adopt the common practice of using the logarithm of capital, and the data much better approximates the normal distribution.

## 3.4. Empirical analysis and discussion

As a preliminary step, Table 3.1 shows the sample distribution of Japanese subsidiaries based on size of equity ownership. We divided subsidiaries (263 samples) into four periods according to year of establishment and by type of equity ownership (majority owned, co-owned, minority owned and full ownership). However, based on this classification (Table 3.1), at least

**Table 3.1:** Sample distribution based on size of equity ownership

| Establishment Year | Number of Subsidiaries | Ownership* | | | |
|---|---|---|---|---|---|
| | | Minority Owned | Co-Owned | Majority Owned | Full Ownership |
| 1954–1980 | 13 | 10 | 0 | 3 | 0 |
| | 4.8% | 76.9% | 0 | 23.1% | 0 |
| 1981–1990 | 37 | 26 | 2 | 9 | 0 |
| | 13.7% | 70.3% | 5.4% | 24.3% | 0 |
| 1991–2000 | 143 | 39 | 11 | 57 | 36 |
| | 53.3% | 27.3% | 7.7% | 39.9% | 25.1% |
| 2001–2006 | 70 | 12 | 3 | 27 | 28 |
| | 25.9% | 17.1% | 4.3% | 38.6% | 40% |
| Total | 263 | 87 | 16 | 96 | 64 |
| | 100% | 33% | 6% | 37% | 24% |

*The values are stated in percentage of firm established in a period with the given mode.
*Note*: Majority owned are subsidiaries which have greater than 50% equity and exclude 100% equity ownership.

recently, multinational companies have tended to acquire a greater equity of ownership. Furthermore, we have four periods according to the establishment of the first Japanese subsidiary to operate in India and until the 1980s which Japan has been one of the largest sources of FDI in the world as well as based on Indian reforms in the 1990s. As Table 3.1 shows, the first investment in India started from 1954 (Sesa Goa Co. Ltd., 51% equity ownership). Of note is that until 1990, Japanese companies had established only 50 subsidiaries. From 1991 to 2000, this number increased to 143 subsidiaries. The number of subsidiaries increased almost threefold during the 1990s. This is likely related to the gradual process of policy change on investment in certain sub-sections of the Indian economy that began in 1991. Modernization, international brands and acquisitions by MNCs have acquired renewed significance in the popular imagination after the reforms initiated by the Indian government in 1991.

According to the information illustrated in Table 3.1, in the years between 1991 and 2000 the percentage of majority-owned subsidiaries is 39.9% while the minority owned is 27.3%. For the last period (2000–2006), the majority owned and full ownership, respectively with 38.6% and 40%, showed the parent companies were interested in keeping a larger equity ownership. It seems Japanese companies were interested in investing in full ownership subsidiaries, based on the sample distribution. As Table 3.1 shows, from 1954 to 1990 there were no full ownership subsidiaries established. Despite the increasing number of subsidiaries, in the two last periods (1991–2000 and 2001–2006) more than 65% (39.9% + 25.1%) and 78.6% (38.6% + 40%), respectively, of subsidiaries had majority or full-equity ownership. Therefore, recently, Japanese multinational companies are more interested in holding the majority of equity of their subsidiaries in India.

Entry strategies in two general categories include wholly owned and joint venture. As shown in Table 3.2, until the 1990s there are no wholly-owned subsidiaries. In total, about 73% of subsidiaries are joint ventures, with the remaining 27% being wholly-owned subsidiaries.

As shown in Figure 3.1, the number of wholly-owned subsidiaries gradually increased from 1980s, while there was no wholly-owned

**Table 3.2:** Sample distribution based on entry strategy

| Period of Establishment | Entry Strategy | | Number of Subsidiaries |
|---|---|---|---|
| | Joint Venture | Wholly Owned* | |
| 1954–1980 | 13 | 0 | 13 |
| | **100%** | **0** | |
| 1981–1990 | 37 | 0 | 37 |
| | **100%** | **0** | |
| 1991–2000 | 103 | 40 | 143 |
| | **72%** | **38%** | |
| 2001–2006 | 40 | 30 | 70 |
| | **57%** | **43%** | |
| **Total** | **193** | **70** | **263** |
| | 73% | 27% | 100% |

*Wholly owned are subsidiaries with 95% or greater equity ownership.

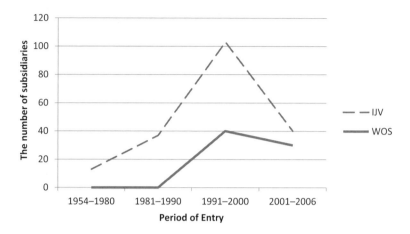

**Figure 3.1:**    The trend of JFDI in India based on entry strategy

*Note*: IJV = International Joint Venture; WOS = Wholly-Owned Subsidiary.

subsidiary in India before this period. However, as India relaxed constraints on high levels of foreign ownership, the MNCs increased their levels of ownership dramatically.

The correlations and descriptive statistics of all the variables in the regression models are reported in Table 3.3. The bivariate correlations show that the year of establishment (subsidiary age) is significantly related to entry strategies, including wholly owned and joint venture. The subsidiary age (SUBA) was negatively significantly correlated (0.307) with entry strategy (ENST) at the 1% significance level, supporting Hypothesis 1 in this study. On the other hand, according to Hypothesis 1, wholly-owned subsidiaries had a positive relationship with subsidiary age.

For this study, we used survival as a dependent variable in order to measure the effect of independent variables on survival. As the results of binary regression, shown in Table 3.4, based on the Model 1, capital had positive significance with a subsidiary's survival.

We had the same result for the effect of the size of the subsidiary on survival, consonant with Ciavarella *et al.* (2004) who show there was a significant relationship between the size of the venture and its survival

Entry Strategies and Survival of MNC's Subsidiaries 59

**Table 3.3 (a):** Pearson correlations matrix for variables

| Variables | 1 | 2 | 3 | 4 | 5 | 6 | 7 | 8 | 9 | 10 |
|---|---|---|---|---|---|---|---|---|---|---|
| 1 SURV | 1 | | | | | | | | | |
| 2 SUBA | -.185** | 1 | | | | | | | | |
| 3 ENST | -.135* | .307** | 1 | | | | | | | |
| 4 INEF | .159 | -.127 | .261 | 1 | | | | | | |
| 5 SUBS | -.058 | .287** | .148* | -.211 | 1 | | | | | |
| 6 CAPL | .112 | -.054 | -.099 | .117 | .253** | 1 | | | | |
| 7 SLSG | .090 | -.116 | -.012 | .039 | -.027 | -.073 | 1 | | | |
| 8 MINO | -.059 | .394** | .397** | -.162 | .174** | -.090 | .008 | 1 | | |
| 9 COWN | -.027 | -.085 | .188*** | -.151 | -.013 | -.026 | .041 | -.203** | 1 | |
| 10 MAJO | .067 | -.327** | -.487*** | .206 | -.155* | .104 | -.025 | -.792** | -.371** | 1 |
| 11 FULL | .140* | -.302** | -.524*** | .120 | -.174*** | .007 | .032 | -.388** | -.174** | .470** |

**Correlation is significant 0.01. *Correlation is significant to 0.05.

*Note:* SURV — subsidiary survival. SUBA — subsidiary age; number of years since the subsidiary was founded. ENST — entry strategy; based on joint venture and wholly-owned subsidiary. INEF — type of industry; industry effect based on manufacturing firms and services. SUBS — subsidiary size; measured by the number of employees in logarithmic form. CAPL — capital; preliminary investment at the time of operation in logarithmic form. SLSG — sales growth ratio; average of five years sales growth. MINO — minority-owned subsidiary; less than 50% equity ownership. COWN — co-owned subsidiary; less than or equal to 50% equity ownership. MAJO — majority-owned subsidiary; greater than 50% equity ownership. FULL — full ownership; subsidiary with 100% of equity ownership.

**Table 3.3(b):** Descriptive Statistics

| Variables | N | Min. | Max. | Mean | Std. Error | Std. Deviation |
|---|---|---|---|---|---|---|
| SURV | 263 | 0 | 1 | 0.726 | 0.028 | 0.447 |
| ENTS | 263 | 0 | 1 | 0.710 | 0.028 | 0.455 |
| MINO | 263 | 0 | 1 | 0.312 | 0.029 | 0.464 |
| COWN | 263 | 0 | 1 | 0.084 | 0.017 | 0.277 |
| MAJO | 263 | 0 | 1 | 0.346 | 0.029 | 0.477 |
| CAPL (LN) | 263 | 11.5 | 22.7 | 17.854 | 0.121 | 1.957 |
| SUBS (LN) | 263 | 0.7 | 8.6 | 4.760 | 0.096 | 1.553 |
| INEF | 263 | 0 | 1 | 0.611 | 0.030 | 0.489 |
| SUBA | 263 | 0 | 52 | 10.734 | 0.469 | 7.614 |
| SLSG | 85 | −0.9 | 8.5 | 0.519 | 0.062 | 1.010 |

**Table 3.4:** Binary logistic regression for Survival and Majority-owned subsidiaries

| Variables | Model 1<br>Subsidiary Survival | Model 2<br>Majority Owned |
|---|---|---|
| Capital | 0.341*(3.390) | 0.205**(6.067) |
| Number of Employees | −0.521**(4.397) | −0.264**(5.670) |
| Subsidiary Age | −0.026***(10.371) | 0.077***(10.640) |
| Full Ownership | 0.660*(2.739) | |
| Type of Industry | | −0.419*(1.802) |
| Constant | −0.811 (0.369) | −155.5***(10.888) |
| **Number of Cases** | **263** | **263** |
| Cox & Snell R Square | 0.253 | 0.146 |
| Chi-square | 14.095*** | 40.619*** |
| Model Coefficients | 0.007*** | 0.0001*** |

*Significant to 0.1. **Significant to 0.05. ***Significant to 0.01.
*Notes*: 1. Numbers in parentheses are Wald Statistics.
2. The dependent variable for Model 1 is subsidiary survival; for Model 2 is majority-owned subsidiary.

in both the logistic regression equation and survival analysis. Therefore, the number of employees as a measure of subsidiary size was negatively ($\beta = -0.521$) associated with a subsidiary's survival, supporting our second hypothesis (H2). The negative value of the number of employees shows that labor costs can have an effect on exit rate. In other words, subsidiaries with a fewer number of employees have a greater likelihood of survival.

The results confirm hypothesis H3, as full ownership (100% of equity) with a value of $\beta = 0.660$ was significantly related to survival. On the other hand, subsidiaries with full equity ownership are more likely to survive. Based on the result of binary regression analysis to examine the impact of age, capital, size of subsidiary and full ownership subsidiary on likelihood of survival, the model can be expressed as:

$$SURV = \beta_0 + \beta_1 CPTL + \beta_2 SIZE + \beta_3 AGE + \beta_4 FULL + \varepsilon$$

where SURV is the subsidiary survival dummy, CPTL is the capital, SIZE is subsidiary size, AGE is subsidiary age, FULL is full ownership and $\beta_i$ is the coefficient of the independent variables. $\beta_0$ refers to the constant and finally $\varepsilon$ is the disturbance term. As the results of Table 3.4 show, the coefficients and Chi-square (14.095) of Model 1 were significant to 1%.

We used Model 2 in order to test hypotheses H4a and H4b. Based on this model, the capital has a positive relationship ($\beta = 0.205$) with the majority-owned subsidiaries. The number of employees related negatively ($\beta = -0.264$) to the majority-owned companies to a 5% significance. In other word, subsidiaries with greater capital and a smaller number of employees are majority-owned subsidiaries. Model 2 shows the subsidiary age has a significant positive relationship effect on majority-ownership, supporting hypothesis H4b. In recent years, MNCs were more likely to operate majority-owned subsidiaries (greater than 50% equity ownership) than minority or co-owned subsidiaries. Thus, based on the results of Model 2, the type of industry ($\beta = -0.419$) has a negative relationship with majority-ownership, refuting hypothesis H4a. On the other hand, subsidiaries in the service industry are more likely to be majority-owned than manufacturing subsidiaries.

Table 3.5 presents the results of linear regression to test the effect of independent variables on the sales growth ratio as a measure of a subsidiary's performance. Model 3 was considered the impact of entry strategy on the sales growth ratio. Based on the results in Model 3, there is no significant relationship between an entry strategy (0.019) and sales growth ratio. However, the results don't support hypothesis H5b, that joint venture subsidiaries are likely to have a greater sales growth ratio than wholly-owned subsidiaries. This model with $R^2 = 0.214$ was significant (0.001) at the 1% level.[2]

---

[2] Although the model's value of $R^2$ is around 0.214, the model is significant at 0.001 level. In addition, the objective of this study is not to include all variables that affect performance, which will give a large number of covariates and consequently increase the level of $R^2$. The aim of this study is to investigate more specifically the effects of firm's factors on performance at subsidiary level, while previous studies focused on this approach on performance at corporate level (Delios & Beamish, 1999; Lu & Beamish, 2001). Furthermore, past studies in the international business, management and economics area, which considered performance as a dependent variable, showed similar levels of $R^2$ in the empirical analyses.

**Table 3.5:**  Linear regression results (sales growth ratio as dependent variable)

| Variables | Model 3 | Model 4 |
|---|---|---|
| Constant | (−1.702)* | (−1.460)* |
| Entry Strategy | 0.019 (0.177) | |
| Subsidiary Age | −0.045 (−0.377) | −0.029 (−0.246) |
| Number of Employees | −0.425*** (−3.169) | −0.394***(−3.004) |
| **Equity Ownership** | | |
| Majority Owned | | −0.046 (−0.166) |
| Co-Owned | | 0.028 (0.182) |
| Minority Owned | | −0.141 (−0.509) |
| **Control Variables** | | |
| Capital | 0.378*** (3.244) | 0.362***(3.123) |
| Industry effect | 0.102 (0.957) | 0.105 (0.975) |
| **Number of Cases** | **85** | **85** |
| R Squared | 0.214*** | 0.227*** |
| Adjusted R Squared | 0.163 | 0.157 |
| df | 5 | 7 |
| F statistic | 4.236 | 3.228 |

*Significant 0.1. **Significant to 0.05. ***Significant to 0.01.
*Note*: The *t* values are in parenthesis.

The result of Model 4 shows, first, no significant relationship ($\beta = -0.045$) between subsidiary age and sales growth ratio. Thus, based on the result, the age of subsidiary as a local experience (Lu & Hebert 2005; Ogasavara & Hoshino 2007b) didn't have an effect on performance and do not support hypothesis H5a in this study.

Second, our results show that there is no significant relationship between majority-owned subsidiaries and sales growth ratio. This implies that the hypothesis H5c cannot be supported.

Third, the number of employees had a negative significant effect on sales growth ratio in Model 3 and 4 ($\beta = -0.425$, $\beta = -0.394$) to 1% significance. Therefore, the number of employees as a measure of subsidiary size is negatively related to the sales growth ratio. On the other hand, subsidiaries with few employees are likely to have a greater sales growth ratio as a measure of performance. Fourth, in both models we found that capital as a control variable (Model 3, $\beta = -0.425$; Model 4, $\beta = -0.394$) had a significant effect on the sales growth ratio, at the 1% level. On the other hand, there is no significant relationship between industry effect (type of industry) and sales growth ratio. As reported in Table 3.5, Model 4 was significant ($R^2 = 0.227$) at the 1% level.

## 3.5.  Conclusions and limitations

In this empirical study, we examine our hypotheses through regression of three dependent variables on our explanatory variables. First, we analyzed the effects of capital, number of employees, subsidiary age and full ownership on the survival of subsidiaries. Our findings show that capital, the number of employees (as a measure of subsidiary size) and full equity of ownership had significant effects on survival. Specifically, subsidiaries with small numbers of employees, greater preliminary capital and 100% equity of ownership have a higher likelihood of survival. Second, we found that when a subsidiary operates in the manufacturing industry, the multinational companies prefer to have a majority of equity ownership. It may be due to assets, export orientation, production technology transfer or future advantages. Also, based on our results, in recent times, the Japanese MNCs prefer to acquire high levels of equity ownership, including full ownership and wholly-owned subsidiaries.

In addition to entry mode selection, according to Dunning's eclectic paradigm (Dunning, 1977; Dunning, 1980; Dunning, 1988), some industry and firm-specific factors, as delineated in ownership and internalization advantages, impact on subsidiary performance. By focusing on one host country and FDI outflow of a single country, the location advantage is controlled (Woodcock *et al.*, 1994; Nitsch *et al.*, 1996). Although the ownership and internalization advantages have been long explored in the conceptual and empirical literature on FDI, multinational firms, and foreign subsidiary performance, most other studies focused on entry mode and performance of subsidiaries established in developed and Asian developing countries.

The ability for a firm to minimize its cost of capital and maximize its availability should be seen as an ownership advantage. A firm that has chosen a proactive financial strategy to achieve this objective has a competitive advantage in future bidding to acquire international assets. This also provides the firm with a partial protection from being acquired by another firm that also has a competitive cost and availability of capital.

As with a foreign subsidiary, the establishment of a joint venture involves the transfer of capital from the home to the host country and must, therefore, be viewed as part of the overall phenomenon of foreign investment. Many host countries consider it important to limit joint ventures to minority participation, rather than foreign majority companies, in order to obtain greater operational control over foreign affiliates. Thus, it may be impossible to establish a wholly-owned subsidiary, and the parent must settle for a joint venture.

Third, we analyzed Japanese subsidiaries' performance based on the sales growth ratio. We found that there is no significant relationship between subsidiary age, entry strategy and equity ownership (especially majority-owned subsidiaries) with sales growth ratio, but the findings suggest that the number of employees as a measure of subsidiary size has an impact on the sales growth ratio. On the other hand, subsidiaries with a small number of employees have a greater rate of sales growth. Therefore, based on this study, subsidiaries with a small number of employees have a greater sales growth rate and thus more likelihood of survival. This implies that cost of human resource is critical for sales growth ratio and subsidiary's survival.

As a measure of size and growth, capital employed was regarded to be more relevant from an entrepreneurship point of view. An increase in the FDI activity has a crowding out effect on local entrepreneurship activity (Das, 2002). Analytically, the study of entrepreneurship in the multinational subsidiary is at a relatively early stage of development. Multinational subsidiary entrepreneurship can be viewed as a developmental process, and therefore the literature on developing subsidiary strategies has considerable significance (Boojihawon *et al.*, 2007). There is a positive relationship between FDI and entrepreneurship. The import competition and FDI discourage entry and stimulate exit of domestic entrepreneurs (Backer & Sleuwaegen, 2003).

This study has several limitations related to its validity and scope. First, the scope of our conclusions is limited to the context of Japanese subsidiaries in India. Second, the data used in this study were from 2001 to 2006. The third limitation is related to the subsidiary data used in this study, published by Toyo Keizai Inc., which has limited data about subsidiaries. Therefore, there are more variables which could affect the results of survival and performance. These problems cannot be avoided since there is only the one source of Japanese subsidiary data available. Nevertheless, our findings illustrate the importance of year of establishment, equity ownership, survival and the sales growth ratio for Japanese subsidiaries in India.

# Chapter 4

# Foreign Ownership, Knowledge Transfer and Parent Firm Specificity

## 4.1. Introduction

As the world's second largest national economy, Japan has long been a highly attractive market for the investors of business and industrial products. However, while many foreign firms maintain a significant presence in Japan, the performance of many others is often disappointing. The failure of foreign investors, including a great number of US firms, in the domestic Japanese marketplace has been attributed to several causes, including demanding and skeptical Japanese buyers, cultural differences, and even discrimination against non-Japanese products (Melville, 1999).

The primary of this chapter is to explore the main determinants of the factors influencing performance of foreign investment in Japan as a developed country, based on an integrative perspective incorporating contingencies at both parent and subsidiary levels. Drawing on primary data from a census of 3500 foreign affiliates, this study makes a number of contributions to the literature on foreign ownership and multinational companies' (MNCs) performance. First, it builds upon prior research by given a comprehensive account of various variables affecting performance, which may be critical to understanding the subsidiary's performance. Second, our research extends existing literature by integrating parent firm factors with the subsidiaries factors. Third, we use several variables to assess the performance, covering different measures of firm performance such as net profit, return on sales (ROS) and return on assets (ROA). Fourth, we compare different aspects of ownership advantages including management and employee levels of foreign investment including the interactions between parent companies and subsidiaries. Fifth, we employed variables like manager authority, foreign manager, new graduate and foreign employees as proxies of knowledge transfer and development.

Researchers have focused on the firm, industry, and country levels of explanatory variables for both home and host country. A review of the equity ownership literature indicates a preponderance of studies focusing on firm characteristics and host country characteristics.

In this context, one of the most important decisions faced by a firm going abroad through a foreign investment is that related to the ownership arrangement, and in particular, the choice between a wholly-owned subsidiary and a joint venture. Many authors refer to this decision as entry mode choice and consider the main alternatives to be full control over the foreign unit (either by acquisition or new creation) or joint ventures with a partner. From now on, we will refer indifferently to entry mode choice or ownership arrangement, in both cases meaning the degree of ownership of the subsidiary by the parent company. Although the ownership and internationalization advantages have been long explored in the conceptual and empirical literature on foreign investment, multinational firms and foreign subsidiary performance, most other studies focused on entry mode and performance of subsidiaries established in developed and Asian developing countries by focusing on one host country and foreign direct investment outflow of a single country.

In this chapter, beside the equity ownership, we focus on a different viewpoint considering the foreign ownership ratio as a key issue for firm-specific factors and knowledge transfer. Mutinelli & Piscitello (1998) maintain that competencies and assets are firm-specific, unique, very difficult to reproduce outside the firm's boundaries and path-dependent. The difficulty of firms in building and acquiring knowledge and competencies influences their growth strategies and in particular, their entry mode and ownership in foreign markets, that is the decision to undertake international joint ventures (IJVs) and alliances rather than establish wholly-owned subsidiaries.

## 4.2. Theoretical background and hypotheses

There are several reasons for studying international modes of entry and ownership. First, the sheer amount of foreign direct investment flows in the world, make it a critical factor in overall economic performance. Second, firms need to identify which host country industry factors are important in choosing among the various modes of entry (joint ventures, acquisitions or greenfield ventures). Third, international diversification through foreign market entry can provide growth and profitability at rates unavailable in home markets. A fourth reason this warrants some attention is the various modes of entry or ownership that can be effectively used to counter international competition by engaging foreign rivals on their home turf.

Fifth, firms have the option of choosing the appropriate entry mode for international markets based on balancing their resources, capabilities, and international experience with their desire for ownership and control. Several studies have examined the performance differences between wholly owned and joint ventures (Nitsch *et al.*, 1996; Pan *et al.*, 1999; Ogasawara & Hoshino, 2007). Finally, equity ownership choices are often massive and irreversible and can influence the long-term performance of the firm (Shrader, 2001). Brouthers' (2002) study of international market entry showed that firms selecting their mode of entry based on the institutional context, transaction costs and cultural context variables should achieve higher entry mode success than firms selecting modes of entry that do not take these factors into consideration. We introduce the following factors into this context.

### 4.2.1. Knowledge transfer

In this study, we employed manager authority, foreign manager, new graduate and foreign employees as knowledge transfer factors.

Research on knowledge transfer has developed out of studies focused on how firms could best accomplish international technology transfers to facilitate pursuit of Vernon's (1966) product life cycle. Early studies found that transfer costs decrease with experience (Mansfield *et al.*, 1979; Teece, 1976, 1977) and examined the speed through which firms are able to first develop and then transfer innovations to subsidiaries (Mansfield & Romeo, 1980; Davidson, 1980). Early conceptual work focused on the role of administrative structures on knowledge flows to and from the rest of the corporation (Bartlett & Ghoshal, 1986). Birkinshaw & Morrison (1995) found that firms with organizational structures that supported combining activities and sharing resources across subsidiary boundaries were more innovative.

Previous studies have provided evidence that a country's knowledge transcends its national boundaries and contributes to the productivity growth of other countries. These studies usually presume particular channels of knowledge transmission (Lee, 2006). Foreign direct investment is also likely to be a significant channel for international knowledge transfer.

The importance of developing and sharing knowledge within the MNC has been stressed by various researchers (Buckley & Carter, 2004; Jensen & Szulanski, 2004; Schlegelmilch & Chini, 2003). The discussion of other researchers focuses on the issue of how to manage the processes of recognizing, developing, and sharing knowledge across subsidiaries worldwide (Foss & Pedersen, 2002; Mudambi, 2002; Yeniyurt *et al.*, 2005). By tapping various kinds of knowledge from the subsidiaries, the MNC can share the existing knowledge and combine this in building new knowledge (Birkinshaw, 2001; Frost, 2001; Hadley & Wilson, 2003). When acknowledging the differentiated MNC, the role of the diverse subsidiaries as creators and contributors of knowledge (Gupta & Govindarajan, 2000) as well as the necessity for MNC subsidiaries to design and choose organizational mechanisms supporting knowledge development and sharing across subsidiaries, must be paid increased attention (Birkinshaw, 2001; Adenfelt & Lagerström, 2006). These considerations suggests our first hypothesis.

**H1a:** *The knowledge transfer factors are positively associated with firm's performance.*

The knowledge-based model is based on an evolutionary view of the firm (Nelson & Winter, 1982) and focuses on cross-border transfer of knowledge. The model understands MNCs as social communities that specialize in the creation and internal transfer of knowledge (Kogut & Zander, 1993). Accordingly, the existence of MNCs is explained by the tacitness and codifiability of knowledge, which make it efficient and effective to transfer a set of capabilities overseas within the same governance structure as that in which the knowledge is embedded. Therefore, MNCs are understood not only as exploiters of their capabilities through knowledge transfer, but also as global learners in the global marketplace (Madhok, 1997).

An important variable that can determine the payoff from foreign ownership is the complementarity of firms' knowledge bases. Learning crystallizes when new information encourages the organization to reexamine its assumptions, combine new knowledge with existing knowledge, or modify its procedures and practices (Zahra *et al.*, 2000). Greater opportunities to acquire, understand and assimilate new knowledge exist when foreign ownership complements rather than substitutes for local knowledge (Hoskisson & Busenitz, 2002). If the recipient firm has the requisite absorptive capacity, it can quickly assimilate and later exploit the knowledge gained from its international ventures. This can facilitate new product and process developments that improve profitability and growth (Block & MacMillan, 1993). Consequently, the acquiring firms that have high absorptive capacity are more likely to benefit from their foreign ownership in gaining superior profits and higher rates of growth (Zahra & Hayton, 2008).

An approach to defining transfer success, termed "knowledge internalization" and adopted in this study, comes from institutional theory (Meyer & Rowan, 1977). It defines success as the degree to which a recipient obtains ownership of, commitment to, and satisfaction with the transferred knowledge. According to Kostova (1999), three factors appear to be related to knowledge ownership. First, greater discretion over the knowledge can allow a recipient to "invest more of their own ideas, unique knowledge, and personal style" in the knowledge (Pierce *et al.*, 2001, p. 301). Second, the intensity of the recipient's association with the knowledge (i.e. the number of interactions involving the knowledge) can affect its feeling of ownership. Lastly, knowledge ownership also relates to the degree that an individual invests energy, time, effort and attention in the knowledge (Csikszentmihalyi & Rochberg-Halton, 1981). Thus, we hypothesize:

**H1b:** *The knowledge transfer factors are positively associated with type of ownership and foreign ownership ratio.*

We employed foreign manager, the number of new graduates employed, the number of foreign employees working in subsidiaries, and the authority of top manager in subsidiary as proxies of knowledge development and transfer.

Pak & Park (2005) proposed that while knowledge transfer played only a marginal role in differentiating the selection of East or West, its effect became stronger when we considered only the two representative target countries, China and the US. This effect deserves consideration because cross-border knowledge transfer is the principal tenet of internalization theory, the knowledge-based approach, and the OLI paradigm. Their results support the notion that the knowledge base of Japanese MNCs exerts a significant influence on their investment activities in the US and China, and further, confirms that Japanese MNCs with a higher level of knowledge development are more actively engaged in the US and West than in China and the East.

Branstetter (2000), using data on patent citations between Japanese investing firms and American indigenous firms, shows that foreign investment is a significant channel for knowledge spillovers, both from investing firms to indigenous firms and from indigenous firms to investing firms. Hanel (2000) approximates the knowledge stock of foreign subsidiaries in 19 Canadian industries as being proportional to the share of sales accounted for by those subsidiaries. His estimation results also indicate that foreign knowledge stocks contribute to Canadian productivity growth; however, the estimated effect of foreign investment from one of his main models is statistically significant only at a 15% significance level.

The MNC motivation for investing in a particular country determines its relative bargaining power with respect to the host and this power balance influences the type of ownership.

Wholly-owned subsidiaries offer firms the highest levels of control, since there is no problem of having to integrate different cultures, divergent strategic view points and separate policies (Nitsch *et al.*, 1996). In addition to entry strategy, according to Dunning's eclectic paradigm (Dunning, 1988), some industry and firm-specific factors, as delineated in ownership and internationalization advantages have impact on subsidiary performance.

Dispatch of personnel from the parent MNC to manage or work in foreign affiliates has often been used as a way to transfer knowledge from parent company to the subsidiary. Firms with more experience in a host country have developed organizational capabilities to that country, which are able to make greater commitments to foreign investments. Makino & Delios (1996) found that local firm's host country knowledge can substitute for the acquisition of local knowledge when the parent has spent a considerable amount of time in the host country.

## 4.2.2. Ownership advantages

The literature on foreign investment has recently analyzed the nature of the firm's entry mode choice in a foreign market, particularly the choice between a joint venture and a wholly-owned subsidiary. The literature on modes of entry is extensive (Pan & Tse, 2000; Brouthers & Brouthers, 2001; Davis *et al.*, 2002). We hypothesize:

**H2:** *A foreign manager will be preferred to a local manager when the firm is wholly-owned or has a majority of foreign ownership.*

Foreign investment in developing countries has maintained relatively stable growth over the period, is concentrated in the tertiary industrial sector, with a higher level of control within a subsidiary, and has been initiated by parent firms with market-seeking and strategic-seeking purposes and with relatively strong ownership advantages (Makino *et al.*, 2004).

The strategy of the parent is proxied by the type of ownership (wholly-owned subsidiary vs. joint venture) and the size of foreign investment venture relative to parent. Modes of entry and equity ownership are key variables in international business research (Li & Guisinger, 1991; Nitsch *et al.*, 1996) and are believed to have a significant impact on performance. They are also an excellent measure for the resources committed to the venture, as well as extent of control exerted by the MNC parent (Woodcock *et al.*, 1994). These considerations lead to:

**H3:** *Wholly-owned subsidiaries and firms with greater ratio of foreign ownership are likely to have better performance.*

The wholly-owned subsidiary (WOS) typically offers the benefits of whole profits and greater control over the operations of a foreign subsidiary. However, since the foreign parent is the sole owner, it must expend greater resources in establishing the operations (Tatoglu & Glaister, 1998). Consequently there is greater downside if the venture fails. Previous studies have argued that, in risky environments, firms often choose other types of ownership over wholly-owned subsidiary (Pangarkar & Lim, 2003). In IJVs, considerable resources need to be spent in finding a partner, and the risks of choosing an inappropriate partner are also borne by the MNC parent. Partners also must work together to integrate different corporate cultures, divergent strategic viewpoints, and policies (Nitsch *et al.*, 1996; Pan & Chi, 1999). In fact, some studies argue that joint ventures are intrinsically inefficient because of the inherently complex management relationships (Woodcock, Beamish & Makino, 1994)

Though there is substantial literature examining the link between entry mode choice and performance, there are several issues with this literature. First, the criteria used by different studies to assess performance have varied across studies. While some studies have examined the degree to which an operation was integrated into the rest of the system, others use factors such as instability, exit rate and longevity. There are several issues with some of the measures employed. Lack of integration into the parent MNC's system may simply be a function of the parent strategic intent for the subsidiary. While control over a subsidiary may be critical to bring about strategic alignment between the parent and the subsidiary, control is hardly an end in itself and hence a problematic measure of subsidiary performance. Other measures such as the amount of exports to the parent also suffer from similar limitations (Pangarkar & Lim, 2003).

### 4.2.3. Parent firm-specific

Previous literature has argued that cultural differences might have a significant impact on the performance of MNC`s subsidiaries (Child, 1994). Makino *et al.*, 2004 research on Japanese investment in developed and less developed countries found that the cross-country differences in financial performance and the exit rate. On the other hand they concluded that the choice of location between less developed countries and developed countries is a key determinant of subsidiary performance. Also, their founding suggests that developing countries provide the environments that reduce the variability of both financial performance and survival likelihood. Therefore:

**H4a:** *The development level of country of origin of the parent company is positively associated with a subsidiary's performance.*

A parent firm's experience in the target market is critical for international expansion, and consequently can have significant effects on performance of foreign subsidiaries (Davidson, 1980). The accumulation of experience helps the parent firm to increase know-how of doing business in the host market and consequently reduce operational uncertainties (Johanson & Vahlne, 1977). This experience can be gained only through learning-by-doing, which is time-consuming.

The lack of international experience may cause the novice investor setting up a wholly-owned subsidiary to take inappropriate decisions on matters such as the choice between producing certain inputs locally or importing them from the parent company, the location of plants in the foreign country, production levels, adaptation of products and services to local market requirements, management of relations with workforce, suppliers, customers, banks, local authorities. Empirical evidence confirms that earlier operations in the target country by the parent company increase the probability of choosing a wholly-owned subsidiary (Mutinelli & Piscitello, 1998). Having a longer presence in the local market allows the firm to interact with a variety of workers, customers, suppliers and other local actors (Zahra *et al.*, 2000).

Furthermore, it helps the firm to know more about the host country and provide more capabilities (Makino & Delios, 1996), to boost know-how for doing business in the market.

The host experience helps MNCs overcome the liability of foreignness and is likely to be positively associated with joint venture rather than wholly owned. However, empirical results about foreign experience effect on entry mode are controversial (Somlev, 2005). We propose the following hypotheses:

**H4b:** *The parent companies with better performance are likely to have subsidiaries with better performance.*

**H4c:** *The higher the parent firms experience in the host market, the greater its propensity to enter using a wholly-owned subsidiary.*

There is a relationship between the size of the parent firm, the entry mode and performance (Brouthers, 2002; Luo & Tan, 1997; Pan *et al.*,

1999; Pangarkar & Lim, 2003). For instance, Hennart & Park (1993) argued that managerial constraints on greenfield expansion might be especially tight when the investor is a relatively small size organization. Larger size MNCs with global reach and an integrated network may facilitate a more effective supply chain (Glaister & Buckley, 1999) further enhancing cost effectiveness of operations and hence leading to better performance. In line with the findings of previous research that foreign parent size impacts on subsidiary performance (Brouthers, 2002; Child *et al.*, 2003; Pangarkar & Lim, 2003; Rihai-Belkaoui, 1998), we hypothesize that:

**H4d:** *The size of parent company is positively associated with subsidiary's performance.*

Entry aiming to acquire resources and complementary assets in foreign markets generally involves greater uncertainty and risk than domestic investments as it requires facing a complex environment where the firm has to deal with many unfamiliar factors. Those reasons induce the firm to commit itself in the costly exercise of gathering and collecting information (Radner, 1992) and influence the internationalization strategy of the firm, particularly its entry mode choice. That is crucial for small-sized firms which suffer from financial and managerial constraints. Constraints and the lack of complementary assets afflicting small-sized firms leave them with few means of reducing uncertainty and force them to resort to co-operative agreements with other (local) firms which enjoy easier access to information channels and assets, as a result of their close network of relations with the surrounding environment. Smaller firms going abroad are then particularly exposed to the risks inherent in foreign investment, because a failure could lead them to bankruptcy. For this reason, they would orient their internationalization strategies towards prudent arrangements, i.e. joint ventures and alliances, in order to minimize risks (Kogut & Singh, 1988; Larimo, 1994).

## 4.2.4. Subsidiary firm-specific

When intermediate market conditions are imperfect, firms have an incentive to bypass them by establishing internal markets (Buckley & Casson, 1976).

Hence, one might expect Japanese MNCs to pursue higher equity ownership in the East because of its imperfect markets. However, Buckley & Casson (1976) stipulate that there are further conditions (i.e. region-specific and nation-specific factors) required to organize an internal market. These are conditions that often fail to obtain in the East, where the social and legal environment imposes strict ownership restrictions, and is permissive to the piracy of patents and proprietary knowledge, and where the political mood is open to at times to expropriation of foreign ownership. In concert, these political and legal constraints and risks discourage Japanese MNCs from organizing the internal markets they might otherwise be motivated to create.

The knowledge-based view seems to make the same prediction; the East has been targeted to exploit standardized technologies, and such a strategic motive usually leads to a lower level of commitment. Dunning's eclectic OLI paradigm also expects that MNCs will avoid full commitment in the East markets, where asset-augmenting activities are rarer than in the West.

The firms demonstrate increased propensity for foreign investment when they are more technology intensive, when their managers have more international experience, and when they are more profitable, controlling for firm size, financial leverage, prior global expansion and home-country currency variation (Trevino & Grosse, 2002)

**H5:** *The size of a subsidiary is positively associated with the ratio of foreign ownership.*

Relative size of the subsidiary is important for two reasons. First, it is a measure for the importance of the subsidiary to the parent; which might, in turn, impact contributions by the parent (Luo, 2001). Greater contributions from the MNC parent in the form of technology or other skills might lead to enhanced revenue potential for the subsidiary. Secondly, relative size also serves as a measure for the competitiveness of the subsidiary due to the presence (or absence) of economies of scale.

**H6:** *Firms with greater import ratios are more likely to be organized as wholly-owned subsidiaries or firms with greater ratio of foreign ownership.*

In general, when foreign firms invested abroad in the same activity, the parent firms are more likely to possess skills, resources and intangible assets that can be transferred to the subsidiaries (Li, 1995). The foreign-owned companies use outsourcing in order to provide required resources as determined by the parent firm. The reasons might be access to the different markets and cheaper raw material, reasonably-priced resources and knowledge or technology transfer.

Kiyota & Urata (2007) found a positive relationship between foreign investment and exports. Also, the multinational firms register faster export growth than domestic firms. They suggested the firms do not choose either exports or foreign investment. Rather, exporters choose whether or not to undertake foreign investment. The foreign investors strongly prefer firms with high export ratios with which they are more familiar on account of their higher foreign sales.

## 4.3. Research design and methodology

The research site was chosen on several grounds. First, Japan is the world's second largest national economy. Second, Japan is an important source of foreign investment research and Japanese foreign investment has one of the largest FDI outflows in the world especially in South Asia and East Asian countries. Third, there are very few studies about foreign-affiliated companies in Japan.

### 4.3.1. Sample and data collection

The empirical study examines the effects of equity ownership, country of origin, managerial skills and employees, based on relationship between parent company specific factors and subsidiary's characteristics, on performance of foreign subsidiaries in Japan.

The primary data source for this study is the Toyo Keizai Inc. Foreign Affiliated Companies in Japan: A Comprehensive Directory (Gaishikei Kigyo), which compiles information on the foreign subsidiaries in Japan that have been established by foreign parents from around the world. The database includes a sample of 3500 foreign subsidiaries established by parent companies from 52 countries covering the period from 2001 up to 2006. A summary of data distribution presented in Table 4.1 based on country of origin and type of ownership. Because of

**Table 4.1:** Distribution of foreign affiliates by country and ownership

| Country | Number | wholly-owned subsidiary | % | IJV | % | Foreign Manager | % |
|---|---|---|---|---|---|---|---|
| America | 1544 | 922 | 60 | 622 | 40 | 356 | 23 |
| Australia | 25 | 14 | 56 | 11 | 44 | 9 | 36 |
| Austria | 20 | 15 | 75 | 5 | 25 | 7 | 35 |
| Belgium | 27 | 16 | 59 | 11 | 41 | 9 | 33 |
| Bermuda | 11 | 11 | 100 | 0 | 0 | 2 | 18 |
| Canada | 46 | 36 | 78 | 10 | 22 | 23 | 50 |
| China | 64 | 38 | 59 | 26 | 41 | 44 | 69 |
| Denmark | 39 | 33 | 85 | 6 | 15 | 16 | 41 |
| England | 263 | 121 | 46 | 142 | 54 | 72 | 27 |
| Finland | 27 | 19 | 70 | 8 | 30 | 12 | 44 |
| France | 270 | 164 | 61 | 106 | 39 | 133 | 49 |
| Germany | 386 | 238 | 62 | 148 | 38 | 123 | 32 |
| Holland | 74 | 48 | 65 | 26 | 35 | 31 | 42 |
| Hong Kong | 62 | 35 | 56 | 27 | 44 | 15 | 24 |
| India | 17 | 8 | 47 | 9 | 53 | 9 | 53 |
| Indonesia | 6 | 3 | 50 | 3 | 50 | 5 | 83 |
| Ireland | 8 | 7 | 88 | 1 | 13 | 2 | 25 |
| Israel | 14 | 12 | 86 | 2 | 14 | 1 | 7 |
| Italy | 70 | 47 | 67 | 23 | 33 | 35 | 50 |
| Korea | 165 | 92 | 56 | 73 | 44 | 132 | 80 |
| Lichtenstein | 8 | 5 | 63 | 3 | 38 | 4 | 50 |
| Luxemburg | 5 | 3 | 60 | 2 | 40 | 1 | 20 |
| Norway | 17 | 10 | 59 | 7 | 41 | 2 | 12 |
| Singapore | 26 | 12 | 46 | 14 | 54 | 7 | 27 |
| Spain | 13 | 6 | 46 | 7 | 54 | 8 | 62 |
| Sweden | 54 | 45 | 83 | 9 | 17 | 20 | 37 |
| Switzerland | 156 | 111 | 71 | 45 | 29 | 57 | 37 |
| Taiwan | 45 | 22 | 49 | 23 | 51 | 22 | 49 |
| Others | 38 | 12 | 32 | 26 | 68 | 15 | 39 |
| **Total** | 3500 | 2105 | | 1395 | | 1172 | |
| *Percentage* | | **60.10%** | | **39.90%** | | **33.50%** | |
| **Mean** | 120.69 | 72.59 | | 48.1 | | 40.41 | |
| **Std. Deviation** | 288.9 | 172.19 | | 117.29 | | 71.94 | |

Note: % is the percentage of each other.

missing data for several variables, the final sample size for the analysis of each variable varied and was reported together with the results of the analysis wherever such a need arose.

As shown in Table 4.1, the United States with 1544 companies, more than 44%, has the greatest number of foreign affiliates in the Japanese marketplace. Germany, France and England respectively with 386, 270 and 263 companies, have large numbers of affiliates in Japan. Table 4.1 presents that from the all foreign affiliates reported in Gaishikei Kigyo, more than 60% (2105) of foreign affiliates are wholly-owned subsidiaries while less than 40% of them are IJVs. Consequently, MNCs tends to acquire greater equity ownership when they have planned to enter in Japanese market.

Also, Table 4.1 presents the number of firms which are organizing by foreign manager based on each country. According to the information illustrated in Table 4.1, it is remarkable that Korea, China and Indonesia have high rates of foreign managership with 80%, 69% and 83% subsidiaries having foreign managers, while only 23% of American subsidiaries, 27% of British and 32% of Germany's subsidiaries in Japan have a foreign manager. This implies that cultural differences and location factors may have a decisive influence on subsidiary management based on employing local managers or foreign managers. This could be due to Western business culture. Also, the location distribution of foreign affiliates in Japan is shown in Figure 4.1. It demonstrates that the United States plus Canada

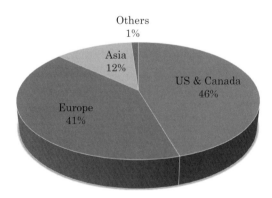

**Figure 4.1:**   Regional distribution of foreign affiliates in Japan

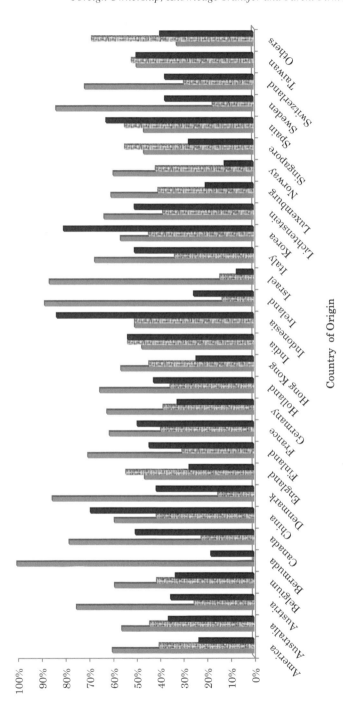

**Figure 4.2:**   The percentage of foreign managers and type of ownership based on country of origin

**Table 4.2:**  Data distribution across industries

| Type of Industry | Number |
|---|---|
| Agriculture | 2 |
| Automobile | 137 |
| Bank | 128 |
| Chemistry | 259 |
| Construction | 17 |
| Consulting | 155 |
| Electronic & electrical equipment | 331 |
| Finance, insurance & real state | 179 |
| Food products | 128 |
| Information service | 171 |
| Machinery | 355 |
| Medical equipment & supply | 151 |
| Other manufacturing | 340 |
| Petroleum | 23 |
| Primary & fabricated metals | 104 |
| Publication | 29 |
| Retail industry | 99 |
| Services | 252 |
| Software | 264 |
| Steel | 6 |
| Transportation | 150 |
| Wholesale trade | 220 |
| **Total** | **3500** |

and European countries respectively with 46% and 41% have a considerable majority of foreign subsidiaries in Japan.

Figure 4.2, however, demonstrate the percentage of foreign manager (number of foreign manager to local manager in subsidiaries) based on country of origin. In addition, it shows the percentage of the type of ownership (JV vs. WOS) of foreign subsidiaries in Japan.

Table 4.2 presents the number of foreign affiliates in Japan based on type of industry. According to the data shown in Table 4.2, MNCs have more investment and greater number of subsidiaries in machinery, electronic and electrical equipment, and other manufacturing industries in Japan.

## 4.3.2. Description and measurement of variables

### 4.3.2.1. *Dependent variables*

For this study, we used several kinds of dependent variable according to hypothesis. The first includes variables which measure the subsidiary's performance. Previous research indicates significant differences in the operationalization of performance with researchers assessing firm performance by measures such as profitability, learning and growth. Consequently, no consensus on an appropriate definition and measurement of performance has yet emerged (Demirbag *et al.*, 2007). Many researchers recognize the inadequacy of traditional measures such as profitability in assessing subsidiary performance (Christman *et al.*, 1999; Pothukuchi *et al.*, 2002; Delios & Beamish, 2004). Since an international subsidiary might perform a variety of roles within the MNCs network, a multifaceted measurement might be more appropriate (Delios & Beamish, 2004; Demirbag & Mirza, 2000; Glaister & Buckley, 1999; Pangarkar & Lim, 2003; Tatoglu & Glaister, 1998). Studies using financial measures of performance indicated that wholly-owned subsidiaries perform better than IJVs, but as Christman *et al.* (1999) argue, financial indicators do not include subsidies and transfer pricing. Furthermore, the magnitude of profit manipulation in many cases is a closely guarded secret. In line with these arguments, we developed three different performance measures, as follows: ROA, ROS and net profit.

ROA represents the profitability of a company relative to its total assets. It gives an idea of how efficient management is to use its assets to generate revenue. It calculated by dividing the company's annual income by its total assets and displayed as a percentage.

ROS is widely used to evaluate the operational performance of the company. It is determined by dividing net profit by sales. ROS is also known as a "operating profit margin". This measurement is useful for management, providing insights on how much profit per dollar generated from sales.

Net profit or net income is calculated by subtracting a company's total expenses from total revenue, thus showing what the company has earned (or lost) in a given period of time. The measure of net profit was computed as averages over the 2001–2006 period.

Second, the dependent variable for ownership is a dichotomous dummy variable constructed based on type of ownership the variable will take a value of zero when the subsidiary's ownership is IJV and will take a value of one when the subsidiary's ownership is wholly owned.

Third, to examine the effect of MNCs and subsidiary's characteristics on ownership, we divided the equity ownership measured by the percentage of equity held by the MNC into three categories: majority owned, co-owned and minority-owned subsidiary. Majority owned is defined as a subsidiary with greater than 50% equity and excluded 100% equity ownership; a subsidiary is co-owned when the equity is equal to 50% and a minority-owned subsidiary has less than 50% equity. If the subsidiary is majority owned, it is coded 1 and 0 if categorized as one of the other types of equity. Fourth, the foreign ownership ratio, which is the percentage of equity owned by foreign affiliates or parent company, has been used as a dependent variable to examine the relationship between foreign affiliated firm-specific and foreign equity ownership.

### 4.3.2.2. *Independent variables*

The independent variables were measured as follows:

Type of ownership: previous empirical researches on subsidiaries have found that wholly-owned subsidiaries outperform joint ventures. Entry mode selection is one of the most important decisions faced by MNCs that are expanding in nations outside their home locations. Wholly-owned subsidiary is a subsidiary in another nation in which the parent company has full ownership and control of the company. IJVs, on the other hand, involve a local and a foreign partner that share the ownership, management, risks and revenue of the new entity. Both wholly-owned subsidiary and IJV entail direct investment in business sites in the target country. In this study, we divided the ownership in two categories and used a dummy variable; a subsidiary is considered to be wholly owned and coded 1 if has 100% of equity ownership by the foreign parent, and otherwise coded 0 as an IJV.

We employed four independent variables in order to define the proxies for knowledge transfer. These variables are foreign manager, number of foreign employees, number of new graduates employed, and manager authority, which defined as follows:

Foreign manager is a non-Japanese manager of the foreign firm's affiliate in Japan. We assume that using a foreign manager instead of local managers for a subsidiary increases the likelihood of knowledge transfer and development between MNCs and their subsidiaries by bringing broad experience and training with him. The existence of foreign manager is a dummy variable that takes a value of 1 if the subsidiary's manager is Japanese and 0 otherwise.

A representative manager should appointed and given authority by parent company to manage, monitor, evaluate and coordinate the subsidiary's activities. Manager authority refers to the formal or legitimate authority specified in a charter giving a top manager the authority to act in the name of the sponsoring executive or on behalf of the organization. A subsidiary's manager position was measured by a dummy variable, which takes a value of 1 if the top position in the affiliated firm is a representative manager who has the appropriate authority to manage the subsidiary, and 0 otherwise.

Foreign employees are the number of foreign persons from parent company or other countries excluding the host country that have been employed to work in an MNC's subsidiary in host market. The variable measured by the number of non-Japanese employees in subsidiary. A subsidiary's intensity of foreign employment is the ratio of foreign employees to total number of employees for each subsidiary.

New graduate refers to the number of new employees in foreign affiliates who are granted an academic degree including college and graduate degrees.

Country of origin is categorized by parent company location. It is measured by using a variable, which takes the value from 1 to 4 to represent each category. We give the value of 1 for United States and Canada, the value of 2 for countries from Europe, the value of 3 for Asia and the value of 4 for the others.

Parent firm size: Several measures have been used by researchers to measure for firm size, e.g. total assets (Yu & Ito, 1988), equity (Cho, 1985), exportation sales and total sales (Kimura, 1989; Agarwal & Ramaswami, 1992), expenditure on R&D (Makino & Delios, 1996) and number of employees (Demirbag *et al.*, 2007, Rasouli & Hoshino, 2007). However, a previous test on the current sample shows that these variables have a high degree of correlation. Because of that, the amount of total assets, sales and parent's employment, were chosen as the indicators of firm size.

We employed parent's sales growth ratio and parent's asset growth as proxies of parent's performance.

The corporation compromises three sets of distinct interests: the shareholders (the owners), the directors, and the corporation officers (the top management). Traditionally, the shareholders control the corporation's direction, policies, and activities. The shareholders elect a board of directors, who in turn selects top management. Members of top management serve as corporate officers and manage the operation of the corporation in the best of shareholders. In closely held corporations with few shareholders, there may be a large overlap among the shareholders, the directors, and the top management. In companies with many shareholders, these are likely to be distinct groups.

The potential separation of ownership from management gives the corporation several advantages over proprietorships and partnerships. (1) Because, ownership in a corporation is represented by shares of stock, ownership can be readily transferred to new owners. (2) The corporation has unbounded life. Because the corporation is separate from its owners, the death or withdrawal of an owner does not affect its existence. (3) The shareholders' liability is limited to the amount invested in the ownership shares.

Import ratio and export ratio variables are determined by the ratio of the amount of import and export from affiliated company to third countries to total sales.

Experience in host country: Makino & Delios (1996) and Delios & Beamish (2001) used the parent company's experience in the host country in logarithmic form as a measure for internalization advantage. It is computed as the log of the total number of years of the company's year of experience in the host country for a foreign investment.

Parent company's experience with the host country may interact differentially in terms of performance (Delios & Beamish, 2004; Uhlenbruck, 2004). Brouthers *et al.* (2000) found a negative relationship between experience and performance, while Luo & Peng (1999) argued that experience leads country-specific knowledge to overcome the liability of foreignness; as a result the firm's performance improves. Given that firms with longer experience considered enjoying greater experiential and tacit knowledge, age is expected to provide a positive relationship with exports and capabilities.

Since the distribution of monetary values usually do not follow normal distribution, the natural logarithm of the values is applied to the total assets, employees and capital of parent companies, in order to smooth the values and to bring them closer to the normal distribution.

Since distributions of monetary values usually do not have normal distribution, the use of natural logarithm of the quantity is applied for parent's total assets, employees and capital, to smooth the values and to bring them closer to the normal distribution. In light of the controversy involving the defining criterion for different sizes, the number of employees, capital and total sales were used as multidimensional measures of the size.

### 4.3.2.3. *Control variables*

Industries are complex entities and multidimensional in nature, and the impact of industry structure on entry strategy and ownership has been relatively unexplored in previous studies. Also, the performance level of firms in one industry may be different from other industries. We included a dummy variable to control industry effects on the performance to avoid biases, coding a value of 1 for manufacturing firms and 0 for service firms.

Considering that other factors may influence the performance of a given subsidiary, the number of employees, capital, total sales and total assets are also applied as control variables for this study.

## 4.4. Empirical analysis and discussion

Table 4.3 presents the correlation matrices and descriptive statistics for the study's variables. As the result of Pearson correlation in Table 4.3 shows;

**Table 4.3(a):**   Bivariate Pearson correlation matrix for variables

| Variables | 1 | 2 | 3 | 4 | 5 | 6 | 7 | 8 | 9 | 10 | 11 |
|---|---|---|---|---|---|---|---|---|---|---|---|
| 1 Type of Industry | 1 | | | | | | | | | | |
| 2 Prior Experience | -0.238** | 1 | | | | | | | | | |
| 3 Type of Ownership | -0.034 | 0.056 | 1 | | | | | | | | |
| 4 Majority Owned | 0.034 | 0.095 | 0.379** | 1 | | | | | | | |
| 5 Co-owned | 0.050 | 0.066 | -0.386** | -0.667** | 1 | | | | | | |
| 6 Minority Owned | -0.097 | -0.184** | -0.346** | -0.610** | -0.157** | 1 | | | | | |
| 7 Country of Origin | 0.065 | 0.033 | 0.094 | 0.031 | 0.030 | -0.072 | 1 | | | | |
| 8 Initial Wage | -0.102 | 0.091 | 0.071 | 0.108 | 0.015 | -0.161** | 0.075 | 1 | | | |
| 9 Foreign Manager | 0.122* | -0.141* | -0.127* | -0.099 | 0.063 | 0.065 | -0.092 | -0.060 | 1 | | |
| 10 Foreign Employees | -0.099 | -0.026 | -0.078 | -0.084 | 0.118* | -0.012 | 0.052 | 0.060 | -0.165** | 1 | |
| 11 Manager Authority | 0.053 | -0.066 | -0.046 | -0.037 | 0.087 | -0.062 | -0.085 | 0.024 | 0.061 | -0.060 | 1 |
| 12 Parent's Assets Growth | 0.026 | 0.011 | -0.011 | 0.004 | -0.030 | 0.024 | -0.113* | -0.035 | 0.071 | -0.105 | 0.040 |
| 13 Parent's Employees | -0.182** | -0.144* | 0.133* | 0.043 | -0.050 | -0.003 | -0.207** | -0.007 | 0.040 | 0.129* | 0.077 |

| | | | | | | | | | | | |
|---|---|---|---|---|---|---|---|---|---|---|---|
| 14 | Employees | −0.171** | −0.362** | −0.122* | −0.101 | −0.119* | 0.249** | −0.177** | −0.106 | 0.024 | 0.288** | −0.063 |
| 15 | Capital | −0.184** | −0.191** | −0.186** | −0.129* | −0.042 | 0.207** | −0.099 | 0.009 | −0.152** | 0.237** | 0.030 |
| 16 | Parent's Sales Growth | 0.053 | 0.016 | −0.064 | 0.032 | −0.027 | −0.015 | −0.050 | −0.023 | 0.055 | 0.088 | 0.035 |
| 17 | Sales Growth | −0.129* | 0.151** | −0.010 | 0.053 | −0.037 | −0.032 | 0.045 | 0.061 | −0.043 | 0.021 | −0.097 |
| 18 | ROA | 0.101 | −0.074 | −0.035 | −0.076 | 0.034 | 0.055 | 0.002 | 0.029 | −0.042 | −0.051 | 0.161** |
| 19 | Net Profit | −0.011 | −0.174** | −0.080 | −0.097 | −0.040 | 0.169** | 0.008 | −0.023 | −0.094 | 0.211** | 0.006 |
| 20 | ROS | −0.191** | 0.082 | −0.008 | −0.052 | 0.019 | 0.039 | −0.055 | 0.085 | −0.058 | 0.059 | 0.108 |
| 21 | Total Sales | 0.041 | 0.041 | −0.023 | 0.061 | 0.005 | −0.085 | 0.008 | −0.018 | −0.030 | −0.017 | 0.048 |
| 22 | Import | 0.299** | 0.034 | 0.322** | 0.197* | −0.146 | −0.133 | 0.165 | 0.204* | −0.197* | −0.111 | −0.129 |
| 23 | Export | 0.215* | −0.075 | −0.003 | 0.006 | 0.002 | −0.017 | −0.105 | 0.000 | 0.137 | 0.096 | 0.016 |
| 24 | Foreign Ownership Ratio | −0.065 | 0.170** | 0.661** | 0.577** | −0.328** | −0.403** | 0.082 | 0.166** | −0.265** | −0.079 | −0.100 |
| 25 | Shareholders | −0.071 | −0.143* | −0.175** | −0.271** | −0.031 | 0.391** | −0.035 | −0.076 | −0.003 | 0.117* | −0.066 |
| 26 | New Graduate | −0.103 | −0.196** | −0.135* | −0.185** | −0.006 | 0.251** | −0.049 | −0.073 | 0.096 | 0.168** | −0.075 |

*(Continued)*

**Table 4.3(a):**   *(Continued)*

| Variables | 12 | 13 | 14 | 15 | 16 | 17 | 18 | 19 | 20 | 21 | 22 | 23 | 24 | 25 |
|---|---|---|---|---|---|---|---|---|---|---|---|---|---|---|
| 1  Type of Industry | | | | | | | | | | | | | | |
| 2  Prior Experience | | | | | | | | | | | | | | |
| 3  Type of Ownership | | | | | | | | | | | | | | |
| 4  Majority Owned | | | | | | | | | | | | | | |
| 5  Co-owned | | | | | | | | | | | | | | |
| 6  Minority Owned | | | | | | | | | | | | | | |
| 7  Country of Origin | | | | | | | | | | | | | | |
| 8  Initial Wage | | | | | | | | | | | | | | |
| 9  Foreign Manager | | | | | | | | | | | | | | |
| 10  Foreign Employees | | | | | | | | | | | | | | |
| 11  Manager Authority | | | | | | | | | | | | | | |
| 12  Parent's Assets Growth | 1 | | | | | | | | | | | | | |
| 13  Parent's Employees | 0.066 | 1 | | | | | | | | | | | | |

| | | 12 | 13 | 14 | 15 | 16 | 17 | 18 | 19 | 20 | 21 | 22 | 23 | 24 | 25 | 26 |
|---|---|---|---|---|---|---|---|---|---|---|---|---|---|---|---|---|
| 14 | Employees | 0.056 | 0.430** | 1 | | | | | | | | | | | | |
| 15 | Capital | 0.057 | 0.348** | 0.611** | 1 | | | | | | | | | | | |
| 16 | Parent's Sales Growth | 0.129* | 0.056 | 0.067 | 0.044 | 1 | | | | | | | | | | |
| 17 | Sales Growth | 0.092 | -0.025 | -0.133* | -0.087 | -0.005 | 1 | | | | | | | | | |
| 18 | ROA | 0.086 | 0.089 | 0.007 | 0.067 | -0.027 | 0.096 | 1 | | | | | | | | |
| 19 | Net Profit | 0.025 | 0.116* | 0.296** | 0.305** | -0.002 | -0.015 | 0.001 | 1 | | | | | | | |
| 20 | ROS | 0.021 | -0.057 | -0.078 | 0.104 | -0.012 | 0.132* | 0.477** | 0.063 | 1 | | | | | | |
| 21 | Total Sales | -0.043 | 0.056 | -0.029 | -0.003 | -0.004 | 0.023 | 0.133* | -0.016 | -0.004 | 1 | | | | | |
| 22 | Import | -0.053 | -0.107 | -0.476** | -0.180* | 0.060 | -0.161 | 0.009 | -0.104 | -0.068 | -0.006 | 1 | | | | |
| 23 | Export | -0.134 | -0.049 | 0.114 | 0.143 | 0.085 | -0.021 | -0.097 | 0.027 | -0.090 | 0.219** | -0.122 | 1 | | | |
| 24 | Foreign Ownership Ratio | -0.096 | 0.024 | -0.140* | -0.094 | -0.008 | 0.043 | -0.032 | -0.044 | 0.062 | 0.027 | 0.382** | 0.054 | 1 | | |
| 25 | Shareholders | 0.107 | 0.106 | 0.289** | 0.285** | 0.004 | -0.005 | -0.014 | 0.578** | 0.071 | -0.027 | -0.113 | -0.053 | -0.163** | 1 | |
| 26 | New Graduate | 0.162** | 0.183** | 0.440** | 0.349** | 0.005 | -0.031 | 0.004 | 0.225** | 0.068 | -0.009 | -0.250** | -0.173** | 0.027 | 0.487** | 1 |

*Notes*: * Correlation is significant to 0.05. ** Correlation is significant to 0.01.

**Table 4.3(b):**   Descriptive Statistics

| Variables | N | Min. | Max. | Mean | Std. Error | Std. Deviation |
|---|---|---|---|---|---|---|
| Type of industry | 310 | 0 | 1 | 0.623 | 0.028 | 0.486 |
| Prior experiences | 310 | 1.6 | 100.7 | 30.654 | 1.039 | 18.295 |
| Type of ownership | 310 | 0 | 1 | 0.474 | 0.028 | 0.500 |
| Majority owned | 310 | 0 | 1 | 0.729 | 0.025 | 0.445 |
| Co-owned | 310 | 0 | 1 | 0.142 | 0.020 | 0.350 |
| Minority owned | 310 | 0 | 1 | 0.129 | 0.019 | 0.336 |
| Country of origin | 310 | 1 | 3 | 1.490 | 0.043 | 0.754 |
| Initial wage | 310 | 176000 | 326000 | 216421 | 1092 | 19235 |
| Foreign manager | 310 | 0 | 1 | 0.752 | 0.025 | 0.433 |
| Foreign employee ratio | 310 | 0 | 0.408 | 0.020 | 0.003 | 0.055 |
| Manager authority | 310 | 0 | 1 | 0.723 | 0.025 | 0.448 |
| Parent assets growth | 310 | −0.645 | 1.312 | 0.128 | 0.011 | 0.189 |
| Parent employees | 310 | 1 | 13.134 | 9.256 | 0.170 | 3.001 |
| Employees | 310 | 0.693 | 10.422 | 5.108 | 0.110 | 1.936 |
| Capital | 310 | 1 | 13.314 | 6.729 | 0.135 | 2.375 |
| Parent sales growth | 310 | −0.911 | 32.340 | 0.226 | 0.105 | 1.850 |
| Sales growth | 310 | −0.900 | 9.821 | 0.169 | 0.048 | 0.838 |
| ROA | 310 | −0.308 | 0.933 | 0.117 | 0.009 | 0.163 |
| Net profit | 310 | −8661 | 512281.0 | 5799.3 | 1810.8 | 31882.4 |
| ROS | 310 | −0.116 | 0.594 | 0.059 | 0.004 | 0.070 |
| Total sales | 310 | 67 | 23691510 | 516880 | 149226 | 2627395 |
| Import ratio | 310 | 0 | 100 | 17.680 | 1.896 | 33.382 |
| Export ratio | 310 | 0 | 100 | 5.284 | 0.811 | 14.283 |
| Foreign ownership ratio | 310 | 20 | 100 | 73.477 | 1.561 | 27.479 |
| Shareholders | 310 | 1 | 197954 | 3446.6 | 1045.2 | 18402.2 |
| New graduate | 310 | 0 | 380 | 12.200 | 2.308 | 40.636 |

country of origin has a negative relationship with the number of parent and subsidiary employees ($p < 0.01$) and parent assets growth ($p < 0.05$). Table 4.3 further shows prior experience in host country is positively associated with subsidiary sales growth and foreign ownership ratio on 1% significant level, respectively. Also, it is negatively associated with parent and subsidiary's employees as well as minority-owned subsidiaries ($p < 0.01$). It implies parent companies that have a longer presence in the local market, do not prefer to enter as an IJV.

According to Table 4.3, foreign manager has negative relationship with type of ownership ($p < 0.05$) and foreign ownership ratio ($p < 0.01$) which states MNCs preferred to have a Japanese manager when the subsidiary is IJVs. Manager authority is one of the knowledge transfer factors, which implies the level of authority acquired by subsidiary in order to make decision, is positively associated with return on assets ($p < 0.01$). However, they partially support hypotheses H1a and H1b.

Table 4.3 shows that there is a positive relationship between the number of foreign employees and net profit at 1% significant level. Thus, firms with greater number of foreign employees had greater profit as a measure of performance. Therefore, it partially supports H1a hypothesis. The type of industry, including manufacturing and services industries, has a positive relationship with import and export ratio at 1% and 5% significant, respectively. Thus, manufacturing firms, as compared to services firms, are more import and export oriented. Also, foreign ownership ratio is positively associated with import ratio ($p < 0.01$) and initial wage ($p < 0.01$), which implies firms with greater ratio of foreign ownership are likely to have greater ratio of import.

As Table 4.4 shows, almost all correlations are low. Therefore, it is good support for thesis H7 in this study.

Tolerance and variance inflation factor (VIF) are examined to determine the existence of multicollinearity. The results of the collinearity test scores show that multicollinearity should not be a problem with these data. However, VIF is less than 3.4 and showed no support for existence of multicollinearity.

**Table 4.4:**    Collinearity statistics

| Variables | Tolerance | VIF |
|---|---|---|
| Type of Industry | 0.64 | 1.6 |
| Foreign Manager | 0.80 | 1.2 |
| Foreign Employees | 0.77 | 1.3 |
| New graduate | 0.59 | 1.7 |
| Manager authority | 0.90 | 1.1 |
| Type of ownership | 0.49 | 2.0 |
| Shareholders | 0.64 | 1.6 |
| Foreign ownership ratio | 0.45 | 2.2 |
| Parent assets | 0.23 | 3.3 |
| Parent sales | 0.23 | 3.4 |
| Parent employees | 0.36 | 2.8 |
| Parent sales growth | 0.93 | 1.1 |
| Parent assets growth | 0.88 | 1.1 |
| Country of origin | 0.90 | 1.1 |
| Prior experiences | 0.77 | 1.3 |
| Initial wage | 0.92 | 1.1 |
| Employees | 0.42 | 2.4 |
| Total sales | 0.70 | 1.4 |
| Capital | 0.60 | 1.7 |
| Sales growth | 0.91 | 1.1 |
| Import ratio | 0.75 | 1.3 |
| Export ratio | 0.86 | 1.2 |

To test the hypotheses, we ran separate regressions analyses. First, as Table 4.5 presents, we ran regression for three measures of firm's performance included ROA, ROS and net profit. The unit of analysis for this part is firm's performance based on financial data available over 2006. From the initial sample of 3500 foreign affiliates, the sample was reduced to 310 cases for analysis of performance. However, because of incomplete data for ROA, ROE and net profit used in this study, we used a final

**Table 4.5:**   Regression results of performance variables

| Variables | ROA | ROS | Net Profit |
|---|---|---|---|
| | | Performance | |
| **1 Industry** | | | |
| Type of industry | 0.103* (1.497) | −0.166** (−1.943) | 0.113(1.142) |
| **2 Knowledge transfer** | | | |
| Foreign manager | −0.034 (−0.597) | −0.007 (−0.104) | −0.018 (−0.228) |
| Foreign employees | −0.170** (−2.017) | 0.154* (1.447) | −0.100 (−0.817) |
| New graduate | −0.011 (−1.133) | −0.056 (−0.523) | 0.329*** (2.692) |
| Manager authority | 0.008 (0.131) | 0.122** (1.700) | 0.044 (0.526) |
| **3 Ownership** | | | |
| Type of ownership | −0.120 (−1.294) | −0.006 (−0.049) | 0.068 (0.511) |
| Number of shareholders | 0.018 (0.288) | −0.055 (−0.714) | −0.007 (−1.077) |
| Foreign ownership ratio | 0.180** (2.098) | −0.098 (−0.895) | −0.071 (−0.564) |
| **4 Parent firm-specific** | | | |
| Parent assets | −1.422*** (−9.186) | 1.227*** (5.165) | −0.067 (−0.218) |
| Parent sales | 1.521*** (8.003) | 0.262*** (2.933) | 0.127 (0.358) |
| Parent employees | 008 (0.079) | −0.060 (−0.494) | 0.136 (0.983) |
| Parent sales growth | −0.011 (−0.183) | −0.145 (−1.932) | 0.108 (1.250) |
| Parent assets growth | 0.115**(1.892) | 0.013 (0.172) | 0.033 (0.377) |
| Country of origin | 0.014(0.233) | −0.016 (−0.222) | 0.092 (1.104) |
| Experience in host country | −0.031 (−0.466) | −0.166 (−1.943) | −0.079 (−0.840) |
| **5 Subsidiary firm-specific** | | | |
| Initial wage | 0.054 (0.973) | −0.006 (−0.090) | 0.079(0.993) |
| Employees | 0.014 (0.151) | 0.049 (0.428) | 0.227* (1.753) |
| Sales | 0.147** (2.439) | −0.133 (−1.261) | −0.272*** (−3.266) |
| Capital | 0.197** (2.343) | −0.197 (−1.846) | 0.235** (1.903) |
| Sales growth | −0.010 (−0.172) | 0.068 (0.966) | 0.062 (0.777) |
| Import ratio | −0.095 (1.306) | 0.108 (1.176) | −0.119 (−1.132) |
| Export ratio | −0.177*** (−2.935) | 0.148 (1.904) | 0.033 (0.913) |
| *Constant* | (−2.137)** | (1.826)* | (−2.082)** |
| Number of cases | **310** | **310** | **310** |
| $R^2$ | 0.768 | 0.634 | 0.533 |
| Adjusted $R^2$ | 0.707 | 0.537 | 0.404 |
| *df* | 24 | 24 | 25 |
| *F* statistic | 12.563*** | 6.559*** | 4.112*** |

\* Significant to 0.1. \*\* Significant to 0.05. \*\*\* Significant to 0.01.

*Note*: The numbers in parenthesis are *t* value.

count of 310 foreign affiliates in Japan for the analysis of firm's performance. We divided the explanatory variables to five categories including industry, knowledge transfer, ownership, parent firm's factors and subsidiary's factors.

As shown in Table 4.5, the type of industry (manufacturing and services) has both positive ($p < 0.05$) and negative ($p < 0.01$) effects on ROA and ROS as performance factors, respectively. From the knowledge transfer variables, foreign employees ($p < 0.1$) and manager authority ($p < 0.05$) have positive relationship with ROS as well as new graduate employee ($p < 0.01$) is positively related to net profit. Also, there is no significant relationship between foreign manager and performance factors. However, they partially support hypothesis H1a in this study.

From the ownership variables, we found only a positive relationship between foreign ownership ratio and ROA on 5% significant level. It is good support for hypothesis H3. On the other hand, subsidiaries with greater ratio of foreign ownership are likely to have better performance. Ramaswamy *et al.* (1998) found that the relationship between ownership control and performance is curvilinear. Contrary to prevailing views that advocate an equal sharing of equity, performance was found to improve with increasingly unequal levels of ownership.

The result of regression shows parent's total assets ($p < 0.01$) and total sales ($p < 0.01$), as proxies of parent's size, are positively associated with ROA and ROS which support hypothesis H5 in this study. Also, the relationship between parent's assets growth and performance is positive with 5% significant level. It is a limited support for hypothesis H4b in this study. Subsidiary's total sales and capital as control variables have positive relationship with return on assets on 5% significant level. Also, capital and total sales as proxies of subsidiary's size have effects on performance. Somewhat surprising, significant negative relationship ($p < 0.01$) has been found between subsidiary's total sales and net profit. Some of the variables including new graduate employee, manager authority, parent assets growth and the number of employees were associated with only one of dimension of performance (ROA, ROS or net profit) providing only limited support for H1a, H3 and H4b hypotheses.

Our results do not provide support for hypothesis H4a. The relationship between performance and country of origin or cultural distance has been discussed by the previous literatures particularly in context of the inherent instabilities of IJVs. Our findings do not provide support for either of the positions (positive or negative). Therefore, the evidence remains inconclusive. Pangarkar & Lim (2003) and Demirbag *et al.* (2007) reached a similar conclusion, although other studies have found a negative association between cultural distance and performance (Li & Guisinger, 1991; Uhlenbruck, 2004).

In the second step of analysis, we used binary logistic regression, as reported in Table 4.6, in order to explore the influence of the independent variables and control variable on the likelihood of either a wholly-owned subsidiary or IJV and equity ownership (majority owned, co-owned and minority owned), we conducted a binary logistic regression analysis. The logistic regression analysis is suitable given the dichotomous characteristic of the dependent variable, and the mix of continuous and categorical independent variables we use (Hair *et al.*, 1995; Dikova & Witteloostuijn, 2007). Before performing the moderations of the ownership variables with a number of independent variables, all predictors were centered to avoid potential multicollinearity problems.

As Table 4.6 presents, foreign manager (F_MNGR) and new graduate (N_GRAD) are negatively associated with type of ownership ($p < 0.01$ and $p < 0.05$, respectively) and minority-owned subsidiary ($p < 0.1$). Further, both have positive coefficient with co-owned subsidiary ($p < 0.05$ and $p < 0.01$, respectively). Therefore, as we expected, parent firms preferred to have a foreign manager for affiliates, when a subsidiary is wholly owned and majority owned. Thus, it supports our hypothesis related to foreign manager (H2). We found only a positive relationship between prior experiences in host country (EXPRNC) and co-owned subsidiary on 5% significant level. However, our findings do not support hypothesis H4c in this study. Parent sales growth (P_SLSGR) is negatively associated with type of ownership and majority-owned subsidiary on 5% and 10% significant level, respectively and has a positive relationship with co-owned equity of ownership.

Based on Table 4.6, parent employees (P_EMPLY) as a measure of size of parent company has positive relationship with type of ownership

**Table 4.6:** Regression results of type of ownership and equity ownership

| Variables | Type of Ownership | | Equity ownership | | | | | |
|---|---|---|---|---|---|---|---|---|
| | | | Majority Owned | | Co-owned | | Minority Owned | |
| INDTRY | -0.918 | 1.215 | -0.375 | 0.248 | 1.401 | 2.182 | -0.059 | 0.044 |
| F_MNGR | -0.900*** | 7.584 | -0.719* | 3.436 | 1.172** | 4.564 | 0.234 | 0.157 |
| F_EMPLY | 0.060 | 0.375 | 0.234 | 1.341 | -0.167 | 0.615 | -0.247 | 0.107 |
| N_GRAD | -0.387** | 7.076 | -0.278** | 6.002 | 0.449*** | 8.440 | 0.234 | 0.386 |
| MNGR_A | 0.645 | 0.955 | -1.364* | 2.593 | 1.999* | 3.107 | 0.279 | 0.214 |
| SHAR_H | -0.001** | 7.290 | -0.002** | 6.588 | -0.001 | 0.657 | 0.001** | 10.313 |
| P_ASSET | 0.252* | 2.371 | 0.091 | 0.260 | -0.107 | 0.290 | 1.521 | 0.051 |
| P_SALS | 1.256 | 0.605 | 1.449 | 0.716 | -0.001 | 0.277 | 1.748 | 0.095 |
| P_EMPLY | 3.101* | 2.827 | 3.678* | 2.552 | -0.001** | 4.614 | 1.828 | 0.462 |
| P_SLSGR | -4.853** | 5.869 | -3.034* | 2.778 | 3.637* | 3.044 | -0.001 | 0.029 |
| P_ASSTG | 4.336** | 4.798 | 1.526 | 0.568 | -1.411 | 0.368 | 0.412 | 0.070 |
| CNTRY | 0.139 | 0.161 | 0.161 | 0.206 | -0.362 | 0.763 | 0.303 | 0.176 |
| EXPRNC | -0.002 | 0.016 | -0.020 | 0.599 | 0.058** | 3.101 | 0.004 | 1.875 |
| I_WAGE | -0.0001 | 1.456 | 5.684 | 0.144 | 1.496 | 0.751 | -0.229 | 0.819 |

| | | | | | | | | |
|---|---|---|---|---|---|---|---|---|
| EMPLYE | 0.001 | 0.611 | 0.006** | 4.136 | −0.009** | 5.850 | −0.01 | 0.097 |
| SALES | 2.602 | 0.044 | −0.0002 | 0.344 | 1.216 | 1.080 | 0.001 | 0.059 |
| CAPTL | −0.193 | 0.756 | −0.166 | 0.522 | 0.244 | 0.819 | 1.828 | 0.046 |
| SALSGR | −0.352 | 0.081 | 1.184 | 0.528 | −1.225 | 0.353 | 0.011 | 0.695 |
| IMPORT | 0.028*** | 13.345 | 0.022*** | 7.515 | −0.022** | 5.995 | −0.004 | 0.016 |
| EXPORT | 0.026* | 3.242 | 0.004 | 0.073 | −0.004 | 0.064 | −1.909** | 2.836 |
| Constant | 6.779 | 0.030 | 38.637 | 0.580 | −21.637* | 3.311 | 0.214 | 1.545 |
| Cases | 310 | | 310 | | 310 | | 310 | |
| Chi-square | 49.715*** | | 31.266** | | 37.047*** | | 37.408*** | |
| −2Log likelihood | 111.096 | | 99.195 | | 81.231 | | 3.814 | |
| Cox & Snell $R^2$ | 0.349 | | 0.236 | | 0.273 | | 0.276 | |
| Nagelkerke $R^2$ | 0.465 | | 0.350 | | 0.428 | | 0.922 | |

* Significant to 0.1. ** Significant to 0.05. *** Significant to 0.01.

*Notes*: 1. Numbers in right sides are Wald Statistics. 2. Majority owned are subsidiaries that have greater than 50% equity and exclude 100% equity ownership. INDTRY, type of industry (manufacturing and services); F_MNGR, foreign manager; F_EMPLY, foreign employees; N_GRAD, new graduate; MNGR_A, manager authority; SHAR_H, the number of shareholders; P_ASSET, total assets of parent company; P_SALS, parent company total sales; P_EMPLY, the number of parent company's employees; P_SLSGR, parent company sales growth ratio; P_ASSTG, parent company assets growth ratio; CNTRY, country of origin; EXPRNC, parent's experience in host country; I_WAGE, the amount of initial wage in subsidiary; EMPLYE, the number of subsidiary's employee; SALES, subsidiary total sales; CAPTL, subsidiary's capital; SALSGR, subsidiary sales growth ratio; IMPORT, import ratio of subsidiary; EXPORT, export ratio of subsidiary.

(wholly-owned and IJV) and majority owned subsidiaries on 1% significant level. Consequently, it implies that parent company with greater size preferred to enter as majority-owned and wholly-owned subsidiaries. The import ratio (IMPORT) is positively associated with type of ownership and majority-owned subsidiary on 1% significant level. However, it partially supports hypothesis H6. In the other hand, wholly-owned subsidiary and IJV with majority owned subsidiary, have a greater ratio of import. As the results in Table 4.6 shows, export ratio (EXPORT) is negatively associated ($p < 0.05$) with minority-owned equity ownership.

The third step of analyses (Table 4.7) tested three regression models. First in the Model 1, subsidiary factors including control variables were regressed on foreign ownership ratio. Second, in Model 2, we added the knowledge transfer factors to the control variables already in model 1 were regressed on foreign ownership ratio. Third, Model 3 illustrates the adapted regression for the all full sample including knowledge transfer variables, subsidiary's factors and control variables.

As the dependent variable in these models is the ratio of foreign ownership and it may not have a normal distribution, we applied a normal score of foreign ownership ratio through using Blom's Formula. Table 4.7 presents, the number of shareholders in Model 1 and 3 are negatively ($\beta = -0.235$, $p < 0.05$) associated with foreign ownership ratio. Kim *et al.* (2007) showed that when a public firm's ownership is concentrated into the hands of a few large shareholders, then these large shareholders should have both the intention and the power to monitor the firm's operations and management effectively. However, while the large shareholder enjoys returns for its monitoring efforts, it also suffers some cost.

Import ratio both in Model 1 and Model 2 has a positive relationship with foreign ownership ratio on 1% significant level. Consequently, there is relatively strong support for H5 with respect to majority equity ownership. As we expected, the results shows that export ratio is negatively ($\beta = -0.251$, $p < 0.05$) associated with the ratio of foreign ownership, supporting our hypothesis H6 in this study. In other words, firms with smaller ratio of foreign ownership and minority owned are likely to have greater ratio of export. Consequently, when the subsidiary is export-oriented,

**Table 4.7:**   Regression models for foreign ownership ratio

| Independent Variables | Foreign ownership Ratio | | |
|---|---|---|---|
| | Model 1 | Model 2 | Model 3 |
| Constant | * (−1.672) | (0.572) | (−1.455) |
| Number of shareholders | −0.204** (−2.318) | | −0.235** (−2.724) |
| Import ratio | 0.431*** (4.495) | | 0.379*** (3.725) |
| Export ratio | 0.082 (0.808) | | −0.251** (−2.048) |
| Initial wage | 0.100 (1.065) | | 0.010 (0.084) |
| Manager authority | | −0.018 (0.186) | 0.586*** (6.071) |
| Foreign manager | | −0.307*** (−3.089) | −0.163 (−1.169) |
| Foreign employees | | 0.058 (0.538) | 3.278*** (3.284) |
| New graduate employees | | 0.236 (1.191) | −1.170*** (−4.582) |
| Control Variables | | | |
| Capital | 0.385** (2.322) | −0.048 (−0.425) | 0.584*** (3.900) |
| Number of employees | −0.353** (−2.268) | −0.415** (−1.996) | 0.821*** (3.466) |
| Total Sales | −0.037 (−0.346) | 0.072 (0.626) | −3.322*** (−3.618) |
| $R^2$ | 0.365 | 0.183 | 0.856 |
| Adjusted $R^2$ | 0.314 | 0.121 | 0.787 |
| df | 7 | 7 | 11 |
| F statistic | 7.159*** | 2.975*** | 12.431*** |
| Number of Cases | 3500 | 3500 | 3500 |

* Significant to 0.1. ** Significant to 0.05. *** Significant to 0.01.
*Note*: The dependent variable is foreign ownership ratio for all three models.

parent firms preferred to have minority-owned subsidiary and limited ratio of ownership.

According to regression results of Model 3, manager authority and the number of foreign employees have positive significant relationship with the ratio of foreign ownership on 1% significant level. Thus, they partially support hypothesis H1b. Contrary to our expectation, new graduate is negatively associated with the ratio of foreign ownership. Finally, based on the results, all control variables have been affected on dependent variable (foreign ownership ratio). Also, based on hypothesis H6, the number of employees and capital as proxies of subsidiary's size, are positively associated with foreign ownership ratio. Consequently, the MNCs preferred to own a greater ratio of equity ownership for larger subsidiaries.

## 4.5. Conclusion and limitations

This empirical study has explored the determination of factors influencing ownership and performance of foreign affiliates in Japan. Findings in this study support the hypothesis that MNCs preferred to enter using a wholly-owned subsidiary in Japanese market.

Our findings offer a number of contributions to the literature. First, consonant with Demirbag *et al.* (2007), we adopt an integrative approach, which incorporates knowledge transfer factors, parent firm and subsidiary variables. Second, we employ a multidimensional measure of performance which enables us to examine subsidiary performance determinants at different views. Third, our findings reveal that impacts of explanatory variables are different on various dimensions of performance. Fourth, our results demonstrate a positive relationship between foreign ownership and some of knowledge transfer factors.

The results on the impact of knowledge transfer and development appear a partially support for our hypotheses. Our findings suggest that manager authority and the number of foreign employees as proxies of knowledge transfer are positively associated with equity ownership. In other words, foreign affiliates in Japan with higher level of foreign ownership are likely to have higher level of management authority and greater number of foreign employees. Therefore, firms with higher levels of ownership control by MNCs (parent companies) are more likely to share and transfer the knowledge.

Our findings indicate that the size of parent company has impact on subsidiary performance. However, larger MNCs had better returns on sales and assets in Japan. As the study of Pradeep & Chhibber (1999) showed, after controlling for a variety of firm and environment-specific factors, only when property rights devolve to foreign owners, at ownership levels providing unambiguous control at 51%, do firms in which there is foreign ownership display relatively superior performance. In case of ROA, we found limited support that parent firm performance has effect on subsidiary's performance. The results shown subsidiaries with greater ratio of foreign ownership had greater returns on assets. Several studies hold that since the entry strategies have specific resource and organizational control demands, the performance of a subsidiary will depend on the selected entry strategies. However, while a study by Vermeulen & Barkema (2001) agrees with the proposition that the entry modes are related to specific levels of resource commitment and levels of control, it does not correspond with the proposition that performance will be directly determined by the selected entry mode.

Contrary to our expectations, country of origin did not affect any of the performance dimensions, which is consistent with Pangarkar & Lim (2003) and Demirbag *et al.* (2007). Also, our findings indicate that foreign manager and parent experience in host country did not have an impact on subsidiary performance. Our findings imply that larger foreign affiliates have better performance in Japanese markets. The evidence demonstrates a negative relationship between export ratio and one dimension of performance. Consequently, export-oriented firms may not exhibit excellent performance in Japan which is a developed country.

The present study holds that both ownership and performance attained by the subsidiary are a direct consequence of the possession or lack of advantages of the parent firms and the subsidiary itself. Consequently, if a parent company possesses enough advantages to overcome the resource commitment and the managerial control costs, it will probably be able to transfer enough capabilities including knowledge to its subsidiary in order to make it generate high performance as well. The evidence provided in this study partly supports the arguments that ownership and parent firm factors may have impact on firm performance. Still, companies that venture through cross-border activities do not always improve their financial performance. This may happen because the integration of acquired firms is time-consuming (Jemison & Sitkin, 1986) and can disrupt the operations of both acquiring and acquired companies (Ahuja & Katila, 2001). Zahra & Hayton (2008) argue that technological knowledge is also usually grounded in national cultures and traditions, inhibiting the transfer of this knowledge. Thus, organizational learning plays a key role in the success of foreign ownerships.

The results demonstrate that wholly-owned subsidiaries and firms with greater ratio of ownership have superior import ratio. However, MNCs preferred to enter and hold minority equity of ownership when a subsidiary is an export-oriented firm. Size of subsidiary had positive impact on foreign ownership. In other words, parent companies preferred to own more equity ownership for large size subsidiaries. Finally, our findings suggest that firms with greater ratio of foreign ownership are supposed to have managers with higher proportion of authority and greater number of foreign employees.

This study is subject to some limitations related to its validity and scope. First, the study covers foreign affiliates only in Japan, while recent studies found stark differences in the characteristics and performance of investment between developed and less developed countries (Makino *et al.*, 2004). Secondly, some of the factors examined in this study may interact with each other. For instance, returns on sales and net profit are both elements of profitability. Also, type of ownership (wholly-owned subsidiary, IJV) and equity ownership are both elements of ownership advantages. When these elements are integrated, they may exert more significant results for ownership and performance. Thirdly, we employed limited number of variables including manager authority, foreign manager and foreign employees as proxies for knowledge transfer and development. Measuring knowledge transfer through these factors may be criticized, as it does not capture location and industry factors. Future studies that use different dimensions to measure knowledge transfer can add to this study in order to improve the validity of related findings.

# Chapter 5

# Industry, Firm-specific Factors and Performance

## 5.1. Introduction

The multinational company (MNC) has several choices of entry mode, ranking from the market (arm's-length transactions) to the hierarchy (wholly-owned subsidiary). MNCs choose internalization where the market does not exist or have poor performance so that transactions costs of the external route are high. The existence of a particular know-how or core ability is an asset that can give rise to economic rents for the firm. These rents can be earned by licensing the firm-specific advantages to another firm, exporting products using these firm-specific advantages as an input, or investment in subsidiaries abroad.

Significant research efforts have been made to examine the importance of firm-specific factors versus industry structure factors in relation to performance variation (e.g. Hawawini *et al.*, 2003; Roquebert *et al.*, 1996). Generally, the effects of firm factors on performance variability have been shown to be more important than industry effects.

Building upon previous research, the present study investigates the importance of firm-specific factors versus industry structure factors. However, here a decidedly different approach is taken. First, the vast majority of foreign firms in Japan come from the United States and Europe. Second, there are very few studies that use asset growth for performance appraisals. Third, we build hypotheses to test key aspects of the firm's factor theories in the stream. Fourth, parent firm factors and subsidiary factors are operationalized and measured to determine their effects on the asset growth ratio (AGR). Lastly, manufacturing versus services firms are compared, which, surprisingly, has rarely been done.

Asset performance means that a company can either earn a higher return using the same amount of assets or is efficient enough to create the same amount of return using fewer assets.

Hymer (1976) proposed that firms exist because they possess unique assets in terms of products, processes and skills. Examples of unique firm-specific assets and intangible wealth include established brand names, the firm's reputation, favored access to suppliers and skilled manpower, and superior products and processes. These resources, when employed in a host country during overseas entry, serve to reduce rivalry, as they are imperfectly imitable. The poor imitability of these unique assets enables a firm to gain competitive advantage or market power over its rivals. Hence, the foreign entrant can be viewed as a special case of the multi-plant firm operating in different countries due to market imperfections (Horaguchi & Toyne, 1990). Such firms integrate industries by owning assets or controlling activities across countries as a result of structural market imperfections and transaction cost advantages.

Nevertheless, foreign firms are likely to be at a disadvantage in terms of understanding the local environment and culture. The international business literature is full of examples of foreign entrants stumbling and failing due to lack of managerial skills or knowledge of local contacts, regulatory issues, political nuances, customer idiosyncrasies and other issues usually unknown to new foreign entrants. These disadvantages are commonly referred to as "liabilities of foreignness."

This empirical study explores first the relationship between type of industry and firm attributes including ownership, experience, import and export ratios, and MNCs' factors. Second, we examined the impact of country of origin, foreign ownership and parent and subsidiary factors on the AGR.

## 5.2. Theoretical background and hypotheses

Firms seeking to establish a presence in the region also faced the decision of how much equity to commit. Empirical studies using cross-country data show that locational and modes of entry choices of MNCs are significantly influenced by host country characteristics. For example, Altomonte (2000) and Bevan & Estrin (2004) use project-specific investment data primarily from European firms, as well as some Asian and US MNCs, to analyze the determinants of foreign direct investment (FDI) to the region. In addition to factors such as country risk and market size, Tihanyi *et al.* (2005) highlight gravity factors and cultural distance as important components of investment decisions. For US firms, advantages such as geographical and cultural proximity are less apparent than for their European counterparts. Yet analyses of market response to early investment announcements by US firms (e.g. Lang & Ofek, 1995) find that, on average, shareholders of US firms experience positive excess returns when they announce expansion plans in transition economies (Paul & Wooster, 2008).

Eclectic theory suggests that in developed countries, wholly-owned subsidiaries have the highest long-term potential (Dunning, 1988). Erramilli *et al.* (1997) found that even the firm-specific advantages of Korean MNCs were dependent on host country location. Therefore, the influence of host country characteristics on entry mode, of which industry structure is an underlying element, is well established.

Previous research suggests that a firm's capacity to earn profits is highly correlated to the attractiveness and profitability of the industry in which the firm operates (Schmalensee, 1989). Hence, when entering an overseas market, a foreign firm will attempt to choose an entry mode that would help overcome industry barriers that might prevent it from succeeding in that overseas market. Therefore, other conditions remaining equal, one would predict that industry characteristics of the host country would play a role in determining a firm's choice of entry mode (Elango & Sambharya, 2004).

### 5.2.1. Industry and firms factors

An important benefit of wholly owned is that a foreign firm can be in control of an established firm, thereby overcoming industry structural barriers in the host country and the liabilities of foreignness rather quickly. Also, wholly owned does not create new industry capacity, as do Greenfield investments, and therefore does not increase industry supply. Wholly-owned subsidiaries of a foreign firm have ownership by a single firm. An international joint venture (IJV) is a partnership wherein the venture (business) is jointly owned by two or more firms. It involves two or more firms investing in or sharing resources, thereby allowing for some degree of flexibility in the sourcing and deployment of resources to overcome industry barriers and minimizing the risks of liabilities of foreignness. While it is hard to accurately predict the influence of a joint venture on industry supply, joint ventures allow for risk pooling, thereby enabling the entrant to more effectively face industry structural barriers and risks due to liabilities of foreignness.

Previous research suggests that a firm's capacity to earn profits is highly correlated to the attractiveness and profitability of the industry in which the firm operates (Elango & Sambharya, 2004). Another notable study was by Caves & Mehra (1986), who looked at 138 entry decisions of foreign firms and considering many industry variables along with firm level variables. The two modes they looked at were mergers and greenfield entrants while controlling for joint ventures. They concluded by claiming that the type of goods produced (durable vs. non-durable), firm size, product diversity and the extent of multi-nationality were likely predictors of acquisition as preferred entry mode, depending on the industry structure (Elango & Sambharya, 2004).

**H1.** *Multinational companies in manufacturing industry are more likely to enter a host market through wholly-owned subsidiaries.*

Companies in different industries face different competitive challenges, causing them to use different approaches to international venturing. When the MNC is diversifying through a FDI, uncertainty and information costs may be higher, so that less control ownership modes should be preferred. Foreign investors are also more likely to enter a foreign market through joint ventures or strategic alliances if they are diversifying into a different industry, as they need tacit industry-specific knowledge, which is subject to relevant transaction costs and it also costly to acquire on the market (Mutinelli & Piscitello, 1998).

Hence, when entering an overseas market, a foreign firm will attempt to choose an equity ownership that would help overcome industry barriers that might prevent it from succeeding in that overseas market. Therefore, other conditions remaining equal, one would predict that industry characteristics of the host country would play a role in determining a firm's choice of entry mode (Elango & Sambharya, 2004).

**H2a.** *Foreign affiliates in manufacturing industry are likely to have a greater number of foreign employees than services industry.*

A common barrier to entry in manufacturing industries is scale economies. Scale economies refer to the need to build a plant at a particular size to produce goods at a reasonable cost. Stated differently, this concept refers to the change in operational costs associated with the change in size of the firm. According to Porter (1980), scale economies arise due to the ability of the firm to perform value activities efficiently at a larger volume. Scale economies are due to lower costs or increased productivity in operations associated with particular levels of production volume.

MNCs need to use their technical employees or expert managers in order to build a manufacturing subsidiary in a host country. Manufacturing firms at the subsidiary level are encouraged to hire a number of the parent company's employees in order to enhance technology transfer and employee training. MNCs build a manufacturing firm and invest in a host market to producing highly-demanded products in host market or compete by offering goods with lower production costs.

When plants are built to scale, the production costs of goods are lowest when operated at capacity (Harrigan, 1981; Scherer, 1980). Industries characterized by a manufacturing structure have significant barriers to entry, as entrants are forced to make significant investments to enter the industry at a particular size. Second, new entrants could face a strong competitive reaction from existing incumbents due to these firms' sunk costs. Third, the creation of new capacity in such industries would hurt all firms, including the entrant. In manufacturing industries, entrance through wholly owned or joint ventures can significantly minimize risk. Therefore, the presence of manufacturing industry requires large investments to be made by the foreign firm, encouraging firms to enter foreign markets through joint ventures or wholly-owned subsidiary.

Elango & Sambharya (2004) argue that in industries characterized by import intensity, firms are likely to prefer wholly owned as an entry strategy. The influence of import on industry profitability and firm behavior is well known in the literature (e.g. Cubbin & Geroski, 1987 and Turner, 1980). Though this variable has not been specifically tested in the entry mode literature, other studies on this topic (e.g. Caves & Mehra, 1986; Porter, 1986) have incorporated import market share in other variables (such as industry concentration) in entry mode models.[1] As this study focuses on type of industry, we decided to test the relationship between the import ratio and industry characteristics. In industries with high levels of import, foreign entrants are likely to use greenfield operations as a favored mode of entry over wholly owned or joint ventures. This will happen because foreign entrants might be more confident in succeeding by setting up operations on their own, considering the fact that they or other foreign firms have had some degree of success selling their products in the host nation (Elango & Sambharya, 2004). This suggests the following hypothesis:

**H2b.** *Foreign affiliates in manufacturing industries are likely to have greater import ratios.*

## 5.2.2. Asset growth

An asset is a business's ability to take productive resources and manage them within its operations to produce subsequent returns. Asset performance is typically used to compare one company's performance over time or against its competition. Possessing strong asset performance is one of the criteria for determining whether a company is considered a good investment.

---

[1]The empirical evidence of short and medium-term impact of foreign investment on exports is mixed. For example, in the case of certain newly industrialized Asian markets such as Chinese Taipei, Singapore, Hong Kong and Malaysia, the consensus seems to be that MNCs have played an important role in export growth (e.g. Kumar, 1996). Moreover, studies of the determinants of FDI location in developing countries indicate that main driving factor is the ease with which enterprises located in the host market can participate in international trade (Sing & Jun, 1995; Kokko *et al.*, 2001). However, broader-based empirical studies generally yield mixed results regarding the role of MNCs in expanding the exports of developing countries (Dunning, 1993; Sharma, 2000).

Analysts use metrics like the cash conversion cycle, the return on assets ratio and the fixed asset turnover ratio to compare and assess a company's annual asset performance (asset growth). Typically, an improvement in asset performance means that a company can either earn a higher return using the same amount of assets or is efficient enough to create the same return using fewer assets.

Hennart & Reddy (1997) reported that joint ventures would be preferred by firms in instances where non-desirable assets are linked with desirable assets, when the Japanese firm has previous experience, when there is good product compatibility, and where there is a growing market. Although these studies found support for the notion that industry structure influences the equity ownership choices of firms, they only used two variables or less to capture that effect.

The ownership advantage explains a firm's resource commitment and refers to assets power that a firm must possess to compete successfully with host country firms in their own markets, which includes tangible and intangible factors such as firm size, multinational experience, proprietary products or technologies, specialized know-how, and skills in innovation and development of differentiated products (Dunning, 1995; Nitsch *et al.*, 1996). The size of the parent firm reflects its capability for absorption of the high costs of marketing, for enforcing patents and contracts, and for achieving economies of scale in foreign markets. Empirical evidence indicates that the impact of firm size on FDI is positive (Cho, 1985; Kimura, 1989). Another form of asset power, a firm's level of multinational experience, has also been shown to influence entry choices (Agarwal & Ramaswami, 1992) and performance (Siripaisalpipat & Hoshino, 2000). As a firm expands its operations overseas, it learns more about how to cope with different environments in terms of economic, political and legal systems as well as the cultural distances. This ownership advantage generates corporate performance (Delios & Beamish, 1999; Gomes & Ramaswamy, 1999), and consequently is reflected in subsidiaries' performance. Finally, intangible assets are necessary to compete efficiently in a certain business line or a given industry (Siripaisalpipat & Hoshino, 2000). A firm will enjoy competitive advantages over its rival if it owns a proprietary product, specialized technology or knowledge, specific know-how, or management capabilities (Kimura & Pugel, 1995).

**H3.** *The greater the ratio of sales growth in MNCs, the greater ratio of asset growth will increase.*

The above hypothesis, in the other words, assumes that the MNCs' sales growth ratio has significantly impact on the ratio of asset growth. One of the measurements for performance appraisal is the rate of sales growth. We assume that the ratio of asset growth is related to its sales growth rate. In other word, the increase of sales growth has an effect on the ratio of asset growth.

Hymer (1976) proposed that firms exist because they possess unique assets in terms of products, processes and skills. Examples of unique firm-specific assets and intangible wealth include established brand names, the firm's reputation, favored access to suppliers and skilled manpower, and superior products and processes. These resources, when employed in a host country during overseas entry, serve to reduce rivalry, as they are imperfectly imitable. The poor imitability of these unique assets enables a firm to gain competitive advantage or market power over its rivals. Hence, the foreign entrant can be viewed as a special case of the multi-plant firm operating in different countries due to market imperfections (Horaguchi & Toyne, 1990). Such firms integrate industries by owning assets or controlling activities across countries as a result of structural market imperfections and transaction cost advantages.

Nevertheless, foreign firms are likely to be at a disadvantage in terms of understanding the local environment and culture. The international business literature is full of examples of foreign entrants stumbling and failing due to lack of managerial skills or knowledge of local contacts, regulatory issues, political nuances, customer idiosyncrasies and other issues usually unknown to new foreign entrants. These disadvantages are commonly referred to as liabilities of foreignness.

**H4.** *Foreign affiliates with more experience in host country are likely to have greater asset growth ratios.*

Experience in the host country may interact differentially in terms of performance (Delios & Beamish, 2004; Uhlenbruck, 2004; Rasouli *et al.*, 2010). Brouthers *et al.* (2000) found a negative relationship between experience and performance, while Luo & Peng (1999) argued that experience leads country specific knowledge to overcome the liability of foreignness. As a result, the firm's performance improves. Given that firms with longer experience are considered to enjoy greater experiential and tacit knowledge, age is considered to provide a positive relationship with exports and capabilities.

Entry in foreign markets and the related uncertainty are also crucial for international neophytes which lack experience in managing foreign operations. The lack of international experience may cause the novice investor setting up a wholly-owned subsidiary to take inappropriate decisions on matters such as the choice between producing certain inputs locally or importing them from the parent company, the location of plants in the foreign country, production levels, adaptation of products and services to local market requirements, management of relations with workforce, suppliers, customers, banks, local authorities (Mutinelli & Piscitello, 1998). Firms acquire increasing capabilities and knowledge about how to manage foreign operations and to correctly assess the risks and the expected economic returns of foreign investment. This is particularly true when the parent company already manages other subsidiaries in that country or if it has entered before other countries which are culturally similar to the country being entered.

**H5.** *Country of origin is significantly associated with the asset growth ratio.*

It is worth mentioning the role of differences in the geographical spread of FDI. Ceteris paribus, high physical and psychical or socio-cultural distance between the parent's home country and the target country engenders high information needs because of the uncertainty perceived by executives and the problems in transferring values, management techniques and operating methods from the home to the host country (Mutinelli & Piscitello, 1998).

Eicher & Kang (2005) present a theoretical model of the multinational firm's optimal entry mode. They show that the choice among FDI, acquisition and exports depends on host country characteristics such as market size, FDI fixed costs, tariff levels and transportation costs. The authors argue that expansion through a sales presence is more likely when firms invest in smaller markets, but as tariffs and transportation costs rise, acquisitions and greenfield investments (such as new plants and wholly-owned subsidiaries) become more likely.

Eclectic theory suggests that in developed countries, wholly-owned subsidiaries have the highest long-term potential (Dunning, 1988). Erramilli *et al.* (1997) found that even the firm-specific advantages of Korean MNCs were dependent on host country location. Therefore, the influence of host country characteristics on entry mode, of which industry structure is an underlying element, is well established.

## 5.3. Research design and methodology

The empirical study examines the relationship between the type of industry entered by MNCs to a host country and type of ownership, import ratio, firm's size and the number of foreign employees. Also, we examine the effect of experience in host country, foreign ownership and country of origin on the AGR.

### 5.3.1. Sample and data collection

The study focused on a broad set of foreign firms in Japan in the both the manufacturing and service industries. Manufacturing firms operated in industries such as food and beverages, textiles, wood and paper products, chemicals, printing and publishing, metal products and machinery. Services firms operated in industries such as construction, wholesale trade, retail trade, transport and storage and business services.

The primary data source for this study was derived from the Toyo Keizai Inc. Foreign Affiliated Companies in Japan: A Comprehensive Directory (Gaishikei Kigyo), which compiles information on the foreign subsidiaries in Japan that have been established by foreign affiliates across the world. The database includes subsidiaries in manufacturing and service industries. However, it includes a sample of 3000 and 500 foreign subsidiaries established by MNCs from 52 countries which covering the period till 2006. A summary of data distribution presented in Table 5.1 based on year of entry, equity ownership and country of origin. From the

**Table 5.1:** Data distribution based on year of entry

| Period | Equity ownership | | | Country of Origin | | | |
|---|---|---|---|---|---|---|---|
| | No. | WOS | IJV | North America | Europe | Asia | Others |
| 1903–1970 | 476 | 207 | 269 | 217 | 205 | 35 | 19 |
| | 14% | 43% | 57% | 46% | 43% | 7% | 4% |
| 1971–1980 | 471 | 263 | 208 | 207 | 201 | 43 | 20 |
| | 13% | 56% | 44% | 44% | 43% | 9% | 4% |
| 1981–1990 | 887 | 527 | 360 | 403 | 371 | 86 | 27 |
| | 25% | 59% | 41% | 45% | 42% | 10% | 3% |
| 1991–2000 | 1002 | 673 | 329 | 460 | 393 | 113 | 36 |
| | 29% | 67% | 33% | 46% | 39% | 11% | 4% |
| 2001–2006 | 664 | 402 | 262 | 293 | 242 | 95 | 34 |
| | 19% | 61% | 39% | 44% | 36% | 14% | 5% |
| Total | **3500** | **2072** | **1428** | **1580** | **1412** | **372** | **136** |
| | 100% | 59% | 41% | 45% | 40% | 11% | 4% |

initial sample of foreign affiliates in Japan, because of missing data for some variables, the final sample size for the research analysis was reduced to 293 cases for the analysis of AGR and type of industry.

Figure 5.1 shows the trends of equity ownership in five periods of foreign investment in Japan till 2006 by MNCs. As shown in Figure 5.1, the number of IJV companies have slump during recent periods. However, the majority of foreign affiliates are wholly-owned subsidiaries. The wholly-owned firms have dramatically increased from 1980s.

As shown in Table 5.1, in the years between 1903 and 1970 the percentage of wholly-owned subsidiaries is 43% while the IJV is 57%. For the period of 1991–2000 and the last period (2001–2006), the percentage of wholly-owned subsidiaries, respectively with 67% and 61%, showed the MNCs were interested in keeping a larger equity ownership of subsidiaries in Japanese market. It seems MNCs were interested in entering via wholly-owned firms, based on the sample distribution.

As the Table 5.1 shows, 85% of foreign affiliates in Japan come from North America (United State and Canada) and Europe with 45% (1580)

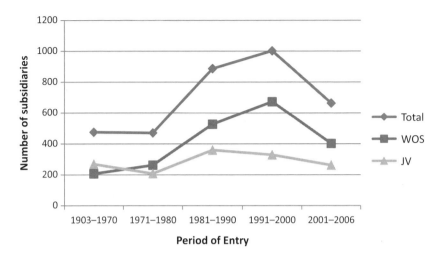

**Figure 5.1:** The ownership of foreign affiliates in Japan based on period of entry

and 40% (1412) respectively. Therefore, recently, MNCs are more interested in holding the majority of equity of their subsidiaries in Japan as a developed country.

As Table 5.2 shows, we find that the machinery industry (10.1%), Electronic & electrical equipment (9.5%), software (7.5%), Chemistry (7.4%) and the other manufacturing industry (9.7) have the higher percentage of foreign investment in Japan.

## 5.3.2. Description and measurement of variables

### 5.3.2.1. *Dependent variables*

Zahra (1991) indicates that companies in different industries face different competitive challenges, causing them to use different approaches to international venturing. The payoff from international venturing might vary also by industry type.

For this study we used two dependent variables. First, the type of industry which is dummy variable coding a value of 1 for manufacturing firms and 0 for the services firms. The second dependent variable is asset AGR was measured by the ratio of average increase in firm's total asset of five years leading to 2006.

**Table 5.2:** Data distribution based on type of industry

| Type of Industry | Number | Percentage |
| --- | --- | --- |
| Agriculture | 2 | 0.1% |
| Automobile | 137 | 3.9% |
| Bank | 128 | 3.7% |
| Chemistry | 259 | 7.4% |
| Construction | 17 | 0.5% |
| Consulting | 155 | 4.4% |
| Electronic & electrical equipment | 331 | 9.5% |
| Finance, insurance & real state | 179 | 5.1% |
| Food products | 128 | 3.7% |
| Information service | 171 | 4.9% |
| Machinery | 355 | 10.1% |
| Medical equipment & supply | 151 | 4.3% |
| Other manufacturing | 340 | 9.7% |
| Petroleum | 23 | 0.7% |
| Primary & fabricated metals | 104 | 3.0% |
| Publication | 29 | 0.8% |
| Retail industry | 99 | 2.8% |
| Services | 252 | 7.2% |
| Software | 264 | 7.5% |
| Steel | 6 | 0.2% |
| Transportation | 150 | 4.3% |
| Wholesale trade | 220 | 6.3% |
| **Total** | **3500** | **100.0%** |

## 5.3.2.2. *Independent variables*

In this study we measured the independent variables as follows:

The first variable is the experience in host country. As in Makino & Delios (1996) and Delios & Beamish (2001), we use the parent company's experience in the host country which is computed as the total number of firm-years of experience in the host country for one foreign investment.

Type of ownership: in this study, we divided the ownership in two categories and used a dummy variable; a subsidiary is considered to be wholly owned and coded 1 if has 100% ownership and otherwise coded 0 as an IJV.

The existence of foreign manager is a dummy variable that takes a value of 1 if the subsidiary's manager is Japanese and 0 otherwise. Foreign employee was measured by the number of non-Japanese employees in subsidiary. The subsidiary's intensity of foreign employment is the ratio of foreign employees to total employees for each subsidiary. New graduate is the number of new graduate employees in the affiliate.

The variable for the country of origin categorized in four regional categories including United State and Canada, Europe, Asia and others based on our data distribution and countries location. It was measured by using a dummy variable for each category which takes the value from 1 if the nationality of foreign affiliate is in the category and otherwise 0.

Several measures have been used by researcher to measure for firm size, e.g. total assets (Yu & Ito, 1988), equity (Cho, 1985), exportation sales and total sales (Kimura, 1989; Agarwal & Ramaswami, 1992) expenditure in R&D (Makino & Delios, 1996) and number of employees (Demirbag *et al.*, 2007, Rasouli & Hoshino, 2007). However, a previous test on the current sample shows that these variables have a high degree of correlation. Because of that, the amount of total assets, sales and parent's employee, were chosen as the indicators of firm size.

We employed parent's sales growth ratio which is the average of 5 years growth rate of parent company's total sales. Import ratio and export ratio variables are determined by the ratio of the amount of import and export from affiliated company.

### 5.3.2.3. *Control variables*

To segregate the effect of firm-specific factors on AGR, we incorporated five control variables into the regression model: three at the subsidiary level and two at the parent firm level. At the subsidiary level, we incorporated capital, gross sales, and the number of employees based on a review of firm variables studied in the foreign investment literature (e.g. Harzing, 2002; Kwon & Konopa, 1992). At the parent's firm level, we incorporated parent's employees and parent's gross sales as control variables based on past research (Hennart & Larimo, 1997). Needless to say, these five variables represent important firm-specific advantages and would play a part in influencing foreign firms' factors towards a greater asset growth. Therefore, they need to be controlled in hypothesis testing.

In light of the controversy involving the defining criterion for different sizes, all control variables in this study can be used as the proxies for the firm's size.

The rationale for the inclusion of firm size is that larger firms are likely to have greater resources and ability to absorb higher risk compared to smaller firms, thereby influencing asset performance differentially.

Table 5.3 shows the name of independent variables used in this study with a short explanation of each variable's definition.

Since distributions of monetary values are typically non-normal, the natural logarithm is applied for firm gross sales and total assets, parent

**Table 5.3:**   Data variables and definition

| Sign | Variable Name | Variable Definition |
|---|---|---|
| EXPRNC | Experience in host market | The number of firm-years of experience in the host country |
| WOS_IJV | Type of ownership | Wholly-owned subsidiary (1) and International joint venture (0) |
| IMPORT | Import ratio | The ratio of import in a foreign affiliate |
| EXPORT | Export ratio | The ratio of export in a foreign affiliate |
| F_EMPLY | Foreign employee | The number of foreign employees working in a subsidiary |
| N_GRAD | New graduate | The number of new graduates in a subsidiary |
| EMPLYE | Employee | The number of employee in a subsidiary |
| P_EMPLY | Parent's employees | The number of employee in parent company |
| F_MNGR | Foreign manager | Manager nationality of subsidiary (Japanese 1 and otherwise 0) |
| P_SALS | Parent's sales | Gross sales of parent company |
| P_ASSET | Parent's assets | Total assets of parent company |
| CAPTL | Capital | The amount of capital of subsidiary |

and subsidiary employees and capital to smooth the values and to bring them closer to the normal distribution as well as to avoid skewness effects.

## 5.4. Empirical analysis and discussion

As a preliminary step, Table 5.4 shows descriptive statistics of the variables and the correlations of all the variables in the regression models are reported in Table 5.5. The results of collinearity statistics are shown in Table 5.6, and there is no support of existence of multicollinearity in the variables of this study.

We used a binary logistic regression for the type of industry analysis. Binary logistic regression is used when the dependent variable is

**Table 5.4:**   Descriptive statistics

| Variables | N | Min. | Max. | Mean | Std. deviation |
|---|---|---|---|---|---|
| Experiences in host market | 293 | 1.6 | 97.9 | 30.027 | 17.182 |
| Type of Industry | 293 | 0 | 1 | 0.642 | 0.480 |
| Capital | 293 | 10 | 385000 | 7958.809 | 31026.799 |
| Type of Ownership | 293 | 0 | 1 | 0.471 | 0.500 |
| Europe | 293 | 0 | 1 | 0.403 | 0.491 |
| Asia | 293 | 0 | 1 | 0.089 | 0.285 |
| Others | 293 | 0 | 1 | 0.058 | 0.234 |
| Import Ratio | 293 | 0 | 100 | 43.157 | 40.307 |
| Export Ratio | 293 | 0 | 100 | 5.621 | 14.634 |
| Employees | 293 | 0 | 14413 | 580.259 | 1318.200 |
| New Graduate | 293 | 0 | 380 | 10.014 | 34.852 |
| Foreign Manager | 293 | 0 | 1 | 0.768 | 0.423 |
| Asset Growth Ratio | 293 | −0.64 | 0.87 | 0.123 | 0.181 |
| Parent's Sales | 293 | 22 | 370998 | 33702.321 | 75563.101 |
| Parent's Sales Growth | 293 | −0.91 | 32.34 | 0.233 | 1.903 |
| Parent's Employees | 293 | 50 | 506000 | 63204.519 | 97729.944 |
| Foreign Employees | 293 | 0 | 102 | 2.645 | 8.242 |

**Table 5.5:** Pearson correlations.

| | 1 | 2 | 3 | 4 | 5 | 6 | 7 | 8 | 9 | 10 | 11 | 12 | 13 | 14 | 15 | 16 | 17 | 18 |
|---|---|---|---|---|---|---|---|---|---|---|---|---|---|---|---|---|---|---|
| 1 Type of industry | 1.00 | | | | | | | | | | | | | | | | | |
| 2 Experience | 0.23 | 1.00 | | | | | | | | | | | | | | | | |
| 3 Capital | −0.23 | −0.05 | 1.00 | | | | | | | | | | | | | | | |
| 4 Type of Ownership | −0.01 | −0.03 | −0.02 | 1.00 | | | | | | | | | | | | | | |
| 5 Europe | 0.03 | 0.10 | 0.09 | 0.12 | 1.00 | | | | | | | | | | | | | |
| 6 Asia | −0.02 | 0.00 | −0.02 | 0.07 | 0.14 | 1.00 | | | | | | | | | | | | |
| 7 Others | 0.00 | 0.00 | 0.00 | 0.06 | 0.27 | 0.74 | 1.00 | | | | | | | | | | | |
| 8 Import Ratio | 0.29 | −0.04 | −0.15 | 0.33 | −0.04 | 0.00 | −0.01 | 1.00 | | | | | | | | | | |
| 9 Export Ratio | 0.24 | 0.10 | −0.06 | 0.01 | −0.09 | 0.00 | −0.01 | −0.18 | 1.00 | | | | | | | | | |
| 10 Employees | −0.08 | 0.25 | 0.18 | −0.12 | −0.05 | −0.06 | −0.03 | −0.22 | −0.01 | 1.00 | | | | | | | | |
| 11 Foreign Employees | −0.09 | −0.02 | 0.06 | −0.10 | 0.06 | 0.02 | 0.00 | −0.11 | 0.03 | 0.34 | 1.00 | | | | | | | |
| 12 New Graduate | −0.16 | 0.10 | 0.18 | −0.17 | −0.04 | 0.06 | 0.10 | −0.24 | −0.06 | 0.58 | 0.15 | 1.00 | | | | | | |
| 13 Foreign Manager | 0.09 | 0.15 | −0.12 | −0.11 | −0.08 | 0.00 | 0.07 | −0.19 | 0.12 | 0.10 | −0.12 | 0.11 | 1.00 | | | | | |
| 14 Parent's Employees | −0.24 | 0.10 | 0.12 | 0.07 | −0.07 | −0.12 | −0.08 | −0.13 | −0.11 | 0.25 | 0.07 | 0.17 | 0.07 | 1.00 | | | | |
| 15 Asset Growth Ratio | 0.03 | −0.03 | −0.03 | 0.01 | −0.21 | 0.01 | 0.02 | −0.05 | −0.07 | 0.08 | −0.13 | 0.16 | 0.09 | 0.05 | 1.00 | | | |
| 16 Sales Growth Ratio | −0.01 | −0.05 | 0.00 | 0.00 | −0.21 | −0.02 | 0.01 | −0.01 | −0.07 | 0.08 | 0.02 | 0.19 | 0.04 | 0.05 | 0.91 | 1.00 | | |
| 17 Parent's Sales | −0.05 | 0.08 | 0.06 | 0.09 | 0.19 | −0.01 | 0.01 | −0.21 | −0.12 | 0.01 | −0.01 | −0.03 | 0.02 | 0.36 | 0.04 | 0.01 | 1.00 | |
| 18 Parent's Sales Growth | 0.05 | −0.01 | −0.01 | −0.06 | −0.07 | −0.02 | −0.02 | 0.06 | 0.10 | 0.04 | 0.10 | 0.01 | 0.06 | 0.13 | 0.14 | 0.14 | 0.09 | 1.00 |
| *N* | 293 | 293 | 293 | 293 | 293 | 293 | 293 | 293 | 293 | 293 | 293 | 293 | 293 | 293 | 293 | 293 | 293 | 293 |

*Notes*: **Correlation is significant at the 0.01 level (2-tailed).
*Correlation is significant at the 0.05 level (2-tailed).

**Table 5.6:** Collinearity statistics.

| Variables | Tolerance | VIF |
|---|---|---|
| Type of industry | 0.709 | 1.41 |
| Experience in Host Market | 0.801 | 1.25 |
| Foreign Ownership Ratio | 0.860 | 1.16 |
| Europe | 0.812 | 1.23 |
| Asia | 0.430 | 2.33 |
| Others | 0.409 | 2.44 |
| Import Ratio | 0.784 | 1.28 |
| Export Ratio | 0.902 | 1.11 |
| New Graduate | 0.615 | 1.62 |
| Sales Growth Ratio | 0.929 | 1.08 |
| Foreign Employees | 0.837 | 1.19 |
| Parent's Sales Growth Ratio | 0.944 | 1.06 |
| Parent's Employees | 0.714 | 1.40 |
| Parent's Sales | 0.759 | 1.32 |
| Capital | 0.581 | 1.72 |
| Employees | 0.309 | 3.23 |
| Gross Sales | 0.307 | 3.25 |

dichotomous, while the independent variables may be of any type. Logistic regression can be used to predict a dependent variable on the basis of continuous and/or categorical independents and to determine the percent of variance in the dependent variable explained by the independents; to rank the relative importance of independents; to assess interaction effects; and to understand the impact of covariate control variables. The impact of predictor variables is usually explained in terms of odds ratios.

Based on the omnibus test result for our binary logistic regression, the model is significant in 1%. Omnibus tests of model coefficients reports significance levels by the traditional chi-square method and is an alternative to the Hosmer–Lemeshow test. It tests if the model with the predictors is significantly different from the model with only the intercept. The omnibus test may be interpreted as a test of the capability of all predictors in the model jointly to predict the response (dependent) variable.

As Table 5.7 presents, the experience in host market (EXPRNC) has a positive significant ($p < 0.05$) with type of industry. The type of ownership (WOS_IJV) and new graduate (N_GRAD) are negatively associated with type of industry ($p < 0.05$ and $p < 0.01$ respectively). It is contrary to our expectation based on hypothesis H1. Therefore, MNCs are interested in holding an IJV when the subsidiary is in a manufacturing industry. In the other words, MNCs in service industry are more likely to enter a host market through wholly-owned subsidiary.

As shown in Table 5.7, the number of foreign employee has a positive significant relationship with type of industry. This supported our hypothesis H2a and implies that foreign affiliates in manufacturing industry are likely to have a greater number of foreign employees than services industry. However, the results show a positive significant relation between foreign manager (F_MNGR) and parent company's gross sales (P_SALS) with type of industry. In the other words, firms in manufacturing industry are more likely to have a foreign manager and greater gross sales.

Our result analysis showed that parent company's total asset (P_ASSET) is negatively associated ($p < 0.01$) with type of industry. It implies that foreign affiliates in service industry are likely to have greater amount of total asset in compare with manufacturing industry.

Larger companies usually have the slack resources for international venturing. Size also gives these firms the market power to preempt competitors' entry and reap higher than normal rates of performance. Conversely, some larger organizations are bureaucratic and therefore slow to adapt to change through international venturing activities (Block and MacMillan, 1993; Hastings, 1999).

To test the hypotheses related to AGR, we ran a multiple linear regression analysis which is shown in Table 5.8. The analyses tested three models. First, in Model 1, all independent variables and one part of country of origin (US & Canada) were regressed on the study's control variables. Second, in Model 2, we added country of origin variables and excluded the parent company factors from the regression model. Third, in Model 3, parent company factors were added to the variables already in Model 2. However, we regressed all variables which can effect on AGR based on our hypotheses.

**Table 5.7:** Binary logistic regression for type of industry.

| Variables | Type of Industry | |
|---|---|---|
| EXPRNC | 0.054** | (3.957) |
| WOS_IJV | −1.335** | (3.302) |
| IMPORT | 0.029*** | (9.053) |
| EXPORT | 0.025 | (1.147) |
| F_EMPLY | 0.100** | (3.748) |
| N_GRAD | −0.24*** | (6.512) |
| EMPLYE | 0.382 | (1.236) |
| P_EMPLY | −0.253 | (1.528) |
| F_MNGR | 1.555* | (2.523) |
| P_SALS | 0.946** | (3.876) |
| P_ASSET | −1.068*** | (4.769) |
| CAPTL | 0.099 | (0.169) |
| Constant | 0.273 | (0.028) |
| **Cases** | **293** | |
| Chi-square | 48.544*** | |
| −2 Log likelihood | 74.579 | |
| Cox & Snell $R^2$ | 0.318 | |
| Nagelkerke $R^2$ | 0.512 | |

*Significant to 0.1. **Significant to 0.05. ***Significant to 0.01.

*Notes*: 1. Numbers in right sides are Wald Statistics.

2. The dependent variable is the type of industry which is a dummy variable coded 1 if the firm is in manufacturing industry and coded 0 if it is in services industry. F_MNGR, foreign manager; F_EMPLY, foreign employees; N_GRAD, new graduate; P_ASSET, parent's total assets; P_SALS, parent's total sales; P_EMPLY, the number of parent firm's employees; EXPRNC, parent's experience in host country; EMPLYE, the number of firm's employee; SALES, firm total sales; CAPTL, firm's capital; IMPORT, the ratio of import; EXPORT, the ratio of export; WOS_IJV, type of ownership (wholly-owned subsidiary and international joint venture).

**Table 5.8:**   The multiple linear regression result of AGR

| Independent Variables | Model 1 | | Model 2 | | Model 3 | |
|---|---|---|---|---|---|---|
| (Constant) | | 1.236** | | 3.074** | | −0.833 |
| Type of Industry | 0.067 | 1.032 | 0.071 | 1.075 | 0.050 | 0.493 |
| Experience in Host Market | −0.019 | −0.290 | −0.036 | −0.544 | 0.188** | 1.871 |
| Foreign Ownership Ratio | −0.074 | −1.218 | −0.067 | −1.095 | 0.172** | 1.707 |
| Europe | | | −0.209*** | −3.363 | −0.257*** | −2.593 |
| Asia | | | −0.015 | −0.169 | −0.099 | −0.685 |
| Others | | | 0.080 | 0.904 | 0.205* | 1.460 |
| US and Canada | 0.192*** | 3.243 | | | | |
| Import Ratio | 0.054 | 0.838 | 0.023 | 0.339 | −0.132 | −1.252 |
| Export Ratio | −0.067 | −1.166 | −0.077 | −1.309 | −0.293*** | −2.970 |
| New Graduate | 0.179*** | 2.703 | 0.169*** | 2.495 | 0.182*** | 2.711 |
| Sales Growth Ratio | 0.121** | 2.101 | 0.131** | 2.227 | 0.124** | 2.135 |
| Foreign Employees | −0.159*** | −2.686 | −0.144** | −2.410 | −0.160*** | −2.696 |
| Parent's Sales Growth Ratio | 0.138** | 2.434 | | | 0.246*** | 2.519 |
| Control Variables | | | | | | |
| Parent's Employees | −0.062 | −0.672 | | | −0.220** | −1.776 |
| Parent's Sales | 0.175 | 1.838 | | | −0.116 | −1.006 |
| Capital | −0.020 | −0.291 | 0.001 | 0.019 | 0.063 | 0.358 |
| Employees | −0.039 | −0.460 | 0.037 | 0.448 | −0.372 | −1.102 |
| Gross Sales | −0.036 | −0.448 | −0.028 | −0.337 | 0.375 | 1.069 |
| $R^2$ | 0.145 | | 0.118 | | 0.282 | |
| Adjusted $R^2$ | 0.101 | | 0.073 | | 0.170 | |
| *df* | 14 | | 14 | | 17 | |
| *F* statistics | 3.313*** | | 2.612*** | | 2.223*** | |
| No. of Cases | 293 | | 293 | | 293 | |

* Significant to 0.1. ** Significant to 0.05. *** Significant to 0.01.

*Note*: 1. The dependent variable is AGR for all three models.

As the results illustrated on Table 5.7, the sales growth ratio in all three models has a significant effect ($p < 0.05$) on AGR on 5% significant level. However, the ratio of parent sales growth is positively associated with AGR. These support our hypothesis H3 in this study which implies that firms with the greater ratio of sales growth are likely to have a greater ratio of asset growth. As Model 3 shows, the experience in host market is significantly associated with AGR. Therefore, it supported the hypothesis H4. In the other words, foreign affiliates with the more experience in host market (older subsidiaries) are likely to have greater ratio of asset growth. As we expected, variables related to country of origin (US & Canada, Europe) are significantly associated with AGR. It implies that the nationality of foreign affiliates has a significant effect on their asset growth rate and this support our hypothesis H5 in this empirical study. Also the new graduate has a positive significant relationship with AGR on 1% significant level.

The regression result Model 3 shows that foreign ownership ratio is significantly associated with the ratio of asset growth. However, the firms with the greater ratio of foreign ownership are likely to have a greater AGR. The ratio of export has a negative significant with the AGR on 1% significant level. Therefore, firms with the lesser export rates have the greater asset growth rates.

Based on the result of multiple linear regression analysis to examine the impact of type of industry, experiences, foreign ownership ratio, country of origin, import ratio, export ratio, new graduate, sales growth ratio, sales growth ratio, foreign employees, parent's sales growth ratio, on likelihood of the ratio of asset growth, the model can be expressed:

$$AGR = \beta_0 + \beta_1 EXPRNC + \beta_2 FOWNR + \beta_3 COUNTRY + \beta_4 EXPORT +$$
$$\beta_5 NGRAD + \beta_6 FEMPLY + \beta_7 SGR + \beta_8 PSGR + \varepsilon$$

where AGR is the asset growth ratio, $\beta_1 EXPRNC$ is the experience in host market, $\beta_2 FOWNR$ is foreign ownership ratio, $\beta_3 COUNTRY$ is country of origin, $\beta_4 EXPORT$ is the ratio of export, $\beta_5 NGRAD$ is the new graduate, $\beta_6 FEMPLY$ is foreign employees $\beta_7 SGR$ is sales growth ratio and $\beta_8 PSGR$ is parent's sales growth ratio and $\beta_i$ is the coefficient of the independent variables. The $\beta_0$ refers to the constant and finally $\beta$ is the disturbance term.

As the results of Table 5.8 shown, all three models were significant to 1% level. International venturing enhances a firm's ability to exploit its existing capabilities and resources while exploring new growth options. Exploitation centers on using the firm's existing knowledge, capabilities and resources in current and new foreign markets (Audia *et al.*, 2000). However, excessive focus on the exploitation of existing capabilities can lead to organizational myopia (Audia *et al.*, 2000; March, 1991) and stagnation. International venturing reduces this risk by promoting exploration activities. Foreign owned companies and international alliances allow the firm to identify emerging technological, marketing and competitive trends in foreign markets. This can stimulate innovation and enhance the variety of the firm's strategic options.

## 5.5. Conclusion and limitations

Our results show a positive relationship between import ratio and type of industry. However, manufacturing firms have higher import in compare with firms in service industries. Contrary to our expectations, the type of ownership is negatively associated with type of industry. In the other words, MNCs in service industry are more likely to enter a host market through wholly-owned subsidiary. The results of industry structure analysis showed that foreign affiliates in manufacturing industry are likely to have a greater number of foreign employees than services industry.

The resource-based theory emphasizes factors internal to the firm. It is argued that acquisition and retention of resources that are rare, non-substitutable and, in combination, difficult to imitate are a source of economic rent and accounts for the heterogeneity of firms in any industry (Reed & DeFillipi, 1990; Mahoney & Pandian, 1992; Oliver, 1997).

According to this view, a company's competitive advantage derives from its ability to assemble and exploit an appropriate combination of resources. Sustainable competitive advantage is achieved by continuously developing existing resources and creating new resources and capabilities in response to rapidly changing market conditions. According to resource-based theorists like Grant (1991) and Peteraf (1993), firms can achieve sustainable competitive advantage from resources like strategic plans, management skills, tacit knowledge, capital, employment of skilled personnel among others. The assets and resources owned by companies may explain the differences in performance. Resources may be tangible or intangible and are harnessed into strengths and weaknesses by companies and in so doing lead to competitive advantage (Saffu & Manu, 2004).

We found that the total assets of the parent company is negatively associated with type of industry. In the other words, firms in service industries are likely to have greater total assets than manufacturing industry. Our findings indicate that experience in host market; foreign ownership and new graduate have a positive and significant impact on AGR. Based on our results, country of origin of foreign affiliates has a significant effect on the ratio of asset growth. Our findings suggest that foreign affiliates from North America including US and Canada outperform subsidiaries from Europe and Asia. In the other words, North American's MNCs have better performance and the ratio of assets growth in Japan. It implies that country of origin matters for assets growth, and that MNCs have various strategies for investment and asset management and consequently, they have different asset performance. However, foreign affiliates from United States have greater AGR versus European subsidiaries in Japan.

Cultural distance is the difference in the values and beliefs shared between investing country and host country. Large cultural distances lead to high transaction costs for multinationals investing overseas (Chen & Hu, 2002) and may limit the effectiveness of behavior-based control mechanisms that rely upon trust, value congruence, and respect (Woodcock *et al.*, 1994).

Therefore, foreign affiliates with greater ratio of foreign ownership and higher experience in host market and greater sales growth rates and lower ratios of export are likely to have greater ratios of asset growth.[2]

This study has several limitations, related to its validity and scope. First, the scope of our conclusions is limited to the context of foreign

---

[2] The direct impact of foreign investment on import falls into two parts, namely an immediate effect emanating from the actual investment and the effects on the import pattern of the targeted enterprises. The former channel is generally limited to the imports of initial inputs of imported machinery and equipment, or of where FDI is large compared with the size of host market; it may include the knock-on effect on aggregate imports from rising total domestic demand. The second channel, which essentially depends on the investor's choice between imported and local inputs, has been studied extensively.

affiliates in Japan. The second limitation is related to the database used in this study which has limited data about firm assets. Therefore, our study covered 293 firms out of 3500 foreign affiliates for analysis of AGR. Third, we employed a subset variables from our database in our analysis of AGR. Therefore, there are more variables which could affect the results of A. Future studies that use more independent variables to measure the asset performance can add to this study in order to improve the validity of related findings.

# Chapter 6

# Conclusions

The purpose of this book was to extend and develop the literature in foreign direct investment, ownership advantages and performance of multinational companies' subsidiaries. The research contributes to the literature by providing empirical support for several theories and previously defined and/or tested constructs. The parent and subsidiary factors measured in this study suggest the importance of internationalization and the ownership advantages of Dunning's eclectic theory. Moreover, according to resource-based theory, the number of employees, capital and total assets constructs measured in this study suggest examining the effect of firm's resources on performance and ownership of foreign affiliates.

Our findings show that foreign affiliates with higher levels of foreign ownership and experience in host market and those with greater sales growth rate and lower export have better performance in terms of asset growth. MNCs especially preferred to acquire high levels of control for large size subsidiaries. We also found that transaction costs play a very important role discovery of efficient and successful market entry strategies. When transaction costs increase, MNCs tend to switch to more hierarchical modes such as wholly-owned subsidiary.

In the first study, we examine FDI and performance of MNCs' subsidiaries in three parts. The first study explores Japanese foreign investment in India. Our findings show that in recent periods, Japanese MNCs prefer to acquire high levels of equity ownership, including full ownership to joint ventures, especially when the subsidiary is in the manufacturing industry. Our results imply that capital and full equity ownership have positive effects on survival. However, the age of the venture and number of employees have negatively effect on survival. Finally we find that subsidiaries with a small number of employees are likely to have a superior sales growth ratio and more likely to survive. This implies that cost of human resource is critical for sales growth ratio and subsidiary's survival.

The second study examines first the impact of knowledge transfer factors, parent firm-specific and subsidiary characteristics on foreign affiliate performance. Second, explore the relationship between firm specific factors and foreign ownership ratio. Based on data derived from 3500 affiliates of MNCs in Japan, the findings show that the factors of industry, foreign employees and size of parent firm and subsidiary generate a statistically significant effect on performance. In contrast, country of origin, foreign manager and experience do not have any significant impact on performance of foreign affiliates. Finally, our findings indicate that manager authority and the number of foreign employees as proxies of knowledge transfer are positively associated with the ratio of foreign ownership. Therefore, foreign affiliates with greater ratio of foreign ownership are more likely to develop and transfer the knowledge in management and employees levels from parent companies. However, supported by resource-based theory, the number of employees, capital and total assets had impact on performance and they demonstrate the effect of the firm's resources on ownership and performance of foreign affiliates.

Moreover, we found that firms with greater ratio of import are more likely to be organized as wholly-owned subsidiary or greater ratio of foreign ownership.

The third study explores first the relationship between type of industry and subsidiary age, export ratio and MNCs' characteristics. Second, examines the impact of country of origin, foreign ownership and parent's specific factors on asset growth ratio (AGR). Our findings show that the factors of foreign ownership, experience in host market, country of origin, export and parent company's sales and the number of employees as a measure of firm size have significantly effect on AGR. The size of parent company has impact on subsidiary's performance. Also foreign affiliates in manufacturing industries are more likely to be organized as an international joint venture (IJV) with a foreign manager and higher ratio of import and greater number of foreign employees. However, contrary to our expectations, we found that firms in service industries are likely to have greater total assets than those in the manufacturing sector. Finally, firms with higher equity of ownership and those in manufacturing industry have superior import ratios. According to transaction cost theory, when a MNC tries to determine whether to outsource or to produce goods or services on its own, the significant factors are including transaction costs, search costs, contracting costs and coordination costs. However, those costs frequently determine whether a MNC uses internal or external resources for products or services.

Notwithstanding its limitations, the study obtained findings that are consistent with the extant eclectic paradigm and resource-based and corporate governance theories and several prior empirical studies. Thus, this research contributes to the literature by providing empirical support for several theories and previously defined and/or tested constructs. For example, the parent and subsidiary factors measured in this study suggest the importance of internationalization and ownership advantages of Dunning's eclectic theory. Moreover, according to resource-based theory, the number of employees, capital and total assets constructs measured in this study propose the effect of the firm's resources on performance and ownership of foreign affiliates.

Our findings show that first, capital, the number of employees (as a measure of subsidiary size) and full equity of ownership had significant effects on survival. Specifically, subsidiaries with small numbers of employees, greater preliminary capital and 100% equity of ownership have a higher likelihood of survival. We had the same result for the effect of the size of the subsidiary on survival, consonant with Ciavarella *et al.* (2004), which showed a significant relationship between the size of the venture and its survival in both the logistic regression equation and survival analysis.

The size of MNCs firm reflects its capability for absorption of the high costs of marketing, for enforcing patents and contracts, and for achieving economies of scale in foreign markets. Empirical evidence indicates that the impact of firm size on FDI is positive (Cho, 1985; Kimura, 1989).

The subsidiaries with a small number of employees have a greater sales growth rate and thus more likelihood of survival. This implies that cost of human resource is critical for sales growth ratio and subsidiary survival. We analyzed Japanese subsidiary performance measured by the sales growth ratio. We found that there is no significant relationship between subsidiary age, entry strategy and equity ownership (especially majority-owned subsidiaries) with sales growth ratio. In our results, contrary to previous studies (Lu & Hebert, 2005; Ogasavara & Hoshino, 2007b), the age of the subsidiary, as a measure for local experience, didn't have an effect on performance. The findings suggest that the number of employees as a measure of subsidiary size has an impact on the sales growth ratio. On the other hand, subsidiaries with a small number of employees have a greater rate of sales growth.

Supported by previous studies (Beamish & Inkpen, 1998; Makino & Beamish, 1998), our findings showed that in recent times, Japanese multinational companies investing in India prefer to acquire high levels of equity ownership and control, including full ownership (100% equity ownership) and wholly-owned subsidiary (more than 95% equity ownership). Most of the host developing countries have developed their policies based on memories of the colonial past when Western firms backed by the colonial governments almost served as agents of imperialism. There is, therefore, an emotional and ideological desire for control reflected in a demand for domestic ownership. A high percentage of foreign ownership is considered undesirable while a significant level of domestic equity ownership is viewed as fair and equitable treatment in terms of incentives to be given to foreign affiliates by the host governments and politics common to all subsidiaries. Other key objectives of host country policies are: developing local entrepreneurship and managerial resources, employment of local nationals at senior managerial levels, saving foreign exchange and promoting exports in order to improve balance of payments, self-reliance, diffusion of shareholding ownership, growth of a capital market, associating local shareholders with the profitability of the foreign affiliates and inducing foreign affiliates into industries of priority or sophisticated technology.

Second, findings in this study support the hypothesis that multinational companies preferred to enter as wholly-owned subsidiary in Japanese market. The results on the impact of knowledge transfer and development on performance appear a partially support for our hypotheses.

Our findings do not provide support for either positive or negative effect of country of origin on performance. Therefore, the evidence remains inconclusive. Pangarkar & Lim (2003) and Demirbag *et al.* (2007) reached a similar conclusion, although other studies have found a negative association between country of origin and performance (Li & Guisinger, 1991; Uhlenbruck, 2004).

Based on our results, firms with larger number of foreign employees are likely to have greater return on sales and lower return on assets.

We found that firms which hold higher levels of control have better performance measured by return on assets. Previous empirical showed that WOS outperform IJV in the developed and developing Asian countries (Woodcock *et al.*, 1994). Kim *et al.* 2007 studied that when a public firm's ownership is concentrated into the hands of a few large shareholders, then these large shareholders should have both the intention and the power to monitor the firm's operations and management effectively. However, while the large shareholder enjoys returns for its monitoring efforts, it also suffers some cost.

As Sengupta (1998) found, the establishment of a joint venture involves the transfer of capital from the home to the host country and must, therefore, be viewed as part of the overall phenomenon of foreign investment. Many host countries consider it important to limit joint ventures to minority participation, rather than foreign majority companies, in order to obtain greater operational control over foreign affiliates. It is, however, an open question whether dilution of foreign holding necessarily means reduction of foreign control. While host countries encourage joint ventures, certain preconditions and infrastructure improvements are essential for their growth.

Our findings suggest that knowledge transfer factors including manager authority, new graduate, foreign manager and foreign employees are associated with equity ownership. In other words, affiliates with foreign manager and higher level of management authority, and greater number of foreign employees, are more likely to share and develop knowledge.

Consequently, as Anand & Delios (1996) stated, the subsidiaries frequently reveal features such as a large number of employees, low amounts of equity, manufacturing activities (rather than service activities) and a greater incidence of joint ventures. On the other hand, subsidiaries in developed countries are usually related to the sale of production and the delivery of services. They are usually wholly owned and require a higher level investment.

Third, our findings indicate that the size of parent company has impact on subsidiary performance. Larger multinational companies had better returns on sales and assets in Japan. As the study of Pradeep & Chhibber (1999) showed, after controlling for a variety of firm and environment-specific factors, only when property rights devolve to foreign owners, at ownership levels providing unambiguous control at 51%, do firms in which there is foreign ownership display relatively superior performance. Fourth, contrary to previous studies, we found an insignificant relationship between ownership and performance. Fifth, multinational companies in manufacturing industry are more likely to invest in a host country as an IJV. Recently, MNCs are interested to enter in a host country as a wholly owned or greater equity ownership.

Sixth, the results demonstrate that wholly-owned subsidiaries and firms with greater ratio of ownership have greater import ratios. However, MNCs preferred to enter and hold minority equity of ownership when a subsidiary is export-oriented. The size of subsidiary has positive impact on foreign ownership. In other words, parent companies preferred to own more equity ownership for larger subsidiaries. Finally, our findings suggest that firms with greater ratio of foreign ownership may be expected to have managers with higher proportion of authority and greater number of foreign employees. Based on our research, when the subsidiary is export-oriented, parent firms preferred to have a minority-owned subsidiary and lower ratio of ownership. As Hennart & Park (1993) found that when transaction costs are low, firms tend to rely on the market to deliver required target market benefits. As the costs increase they tend to switch to more hierarchical modes e.g. wholly-owned subsidiaries. The core dimensions of these transactions are the asset specificity, the frequency of economic exchange, and uncertainty surrounding the exchange of resources between the focal parties.

Our finding showed that multinational companies in service industry are more likely to enter a host market through wholly-owned subsidiary.

The results of industry structure analysis showed that foreign affiliates in manufacturing industry are likely to have a greater number of foreign employees than services industry.

Based on our results, country of origin of foreign affiliates has a significant effect on the ratio of asset growth. In the other words, multinational companies from different country have different strategy to invest and asset management as well as different asset performance. Our study shows that foreign affiliates from United States have greater AGR versus European subsidiaries in Japan. Therefore, foreign affiliates with greater ratio of foreign ownership and higher experience in host market and greater sales growth rate and lower ratio of export are likely to have greater ratio of asset growth.

We found a positive relationship between firm assets and sales with firm's performance. Therefore, consistent with resource-based view (Grant, 1991; Peteraf, 1993), firms can achieve sustainable competitive advantage from resources like strategic plans, management skills, tacit knowledge, capital, employment of skilled personnel among others. The assets and resources owned by companies may explain the differences in performance. Resources may be tangible or intangible and are harnessed into strengths and weaknesses by companies and in so doing lead to competitive advantage.

Our finding is consistent with the OLI paradigm (Dunning's eclectic theory). It posits that a firm will invest overseas when it has either an ownership advantages (trademark, production technique, entrepreneurship skills, returns to scale, shareholders), or the intended investment site has a locational attraction (existence of raw materials, low wages, special taxes or tariffs), and the firm prefers to internalize these advantages by producing abroad, as opposed to indirectly profiting from its advantages by producing through a partnership arrangement such as licensing or a joint venture. An organizational advantage facilitates the transference of technology or some special skills and in some sense is an exportation of a service. As such, foreign investment improves the overall welfare of both the sending and the recipient countries, while still having distributional effects. However, in this theoretical model, not all the net impacts associated with foreign investment are positive.

Our findings suggest that foreign affiliates from North America including US and Canada outperform subsidiaries from Europe and Asia.

In the other words, North American multinational companies have better performance measured by the ratio of assets growth in Japan. It implies that country of origin matters for assets growth and MNCs have different strategy to invest and asset management.

The ownership advantage explains a firm's resource commitment and refers to assets that a firm must possess to compete successfully with host country firms in their own markets, which can be tangible or intangible, such as firm size, multinational experience, proprietary products or technologies, specialized know-how, or skills in innovation or development of differentiated products (Dunning, 1993; Dunning, 1995; Nitsch *et al.*, 1996). Another form of asset, a firm's level of multinational experience, has also been shown to influence entry choices (Agarwal & Ramaswami, 1992) and performance (Siripaisalpipat & Hoshino, 2000). As a firm expands its operations overseas, it learns more about how to cope with different environment in terms of economic, political, and legal systems as well as the cultural distances. This ownership advantage generated corporate performance (Delios & Beamish, 1999; Gomes & Ramaswamy, 1999), and consequently is reflected in subsidiary performance.

The resource-based view posits that a firm's sustainable competitive advantage is reached by virtue of unique resources which these resources have the characteristics of being rare, valuable, inimitable, non-tradable and non-substitutable as well as firm specific.

The MNCs have to handle and control multiple transactions in remote locations adopting a variety of coordination mechanisms most of which have been invented for the purpose of effective administration and management of economic activities in organizations and institutions. The complexity of MNC operations requires a complex set of tools used by individual and collective agents all engaged in a complex allocation of resources for operational and strategic purposes. In this context the discussion of the decision-making power of the individual members of the board of directors, or the accountability of insider agents to outsider shareholders and stakeholders merely reaches the paradox that there are no boundaries to managerial opportunism, and enhanced control that assumes tentative opportunism, generates merely more sophisticated evasive manoeuvres from executives entrusted to handle operational risks.

Policy makers in some emerging markets tend to see foreign investment as a possible vehicle for raising exports. The prevailing reasoning is that MNCs may increase the export orientation of domestic market through channels that include: their higher degree of sophistication in product quality, brand recognition and access to world markets; their potential for alleviating constraints on the use of the host market's factor endowment; and their longer-term impact on the international competitiveness of the host market business sector.

This study has several limitations, related to its validity and scope. First, the scope of our conclusions is limited to the context of Japanese subsidiaries in India and foreign affiliates in Japan. Second, the data used in this study were from 2001 to 2006. The third limitation is related to the subsidiary data used in this study, published by Toyo Keizai Inc., which has limited data about subsidiaries. Therefore, there are more variables which could affect the results of survival and performance. These problems cannot be avoided since there is only the one source of Japanese subsidiary data available. Nevertheless, our findings illustrate the importance of year of establishment, equity ownership, survival and the sales growth ratio for Japanese subsidiaries in India.

Fourth, since the study covers foreign affiliates in Japan. The recent studies found stark differences in the characteristics and performance of investment between developed and less developed countries (Makino *et al.*, 2004). Fifth, we employed limited number of variables including manager authority, foreign manager and foreign employees as proxies for knowledge transfer and development. Measuring knowledge transfer through these factors may be criticized, as it does not capture location and industry factors. Future studies that use different dimensions to measure knowledge transfer can add to this study in order to improve the validity of related findings.

# References

Adenfelt, M. & Lagerströmb, K., 2006. Knowledge development and sharing in multinational corporations: The case of a centre of excellence and a transnational team. *International Business Review*, 12, 381–400.

Agarwal, J.P., 1980. Determinants of foreign direct investment: A survey. *Weltwirtschaftliches Archiv*, 116(4), 739–773.

Agarwal, S. & Ramaswami, S.N., 1992. Choice of foreign market entry mode: Impact of ownership, location and internalization factors. *Journal of International Business Studies*, 23(1), 1–28.

Aharoni, Y., 1966. *The Foreign Investment Decision Process*. Harvard Business School Press, Boston, MA.

Ahuja, G. & Katila, R., 2001. Technological acquisitions and the innovation performance of acquiring firms: A longitudinal study. *Strategic Management Journal*, 22(3), 197–220.

Altomonte C., 2000. Economic determinants and institutional frameworks: FDI in economies in transition. *Transnational Corporations*, 9(2), 75–106.

Anand, J. & Delios, A., 1996. Competing globally: How Japanese MNCs have matched goals and strategies in India and China. *The Columbia Journal of World Business*, 31(3), 50–62.

Andersen, O., 1997. Internalization and market entry mode: A review of theories and conceptual frameworks. *Management International Review*, 37 (Special Issue), 27–42.

Audia, P.G., Locke, E.A., & Smith, K.G., 2000. The paradox of success: An archival and a laboratory study of strategic persistence following radical environmental change. *Academy of Management Journal*, 43(5), 837–853.

Backer, D.K. & Sleuwaegen, L., 2003. Does foreign direct investment crowd out domestic entrepreneurship? *Review of Industrial Organization*, 22, 67–84.

Baranson, J., 1970, Technology transfer through the international firm. *American Economic Review Papers and Proceedings*, 60(2), 435–441.

Barlow, E.R., & Wender, I.T., 1955. *Foreign Investment and Taxation*, Prentice-Hall Inc., Englewood Cliffs, N.J.

Barney, J.B., 1991. Firm resources and sustained competitive advantages. *Journal of Management*, 17(1), 99–120.

Bartlett, C.A., & Ghoshal, S., 1986. Tap your subsidiaries for global reach. *Harvard Business Review*, 64(6), 87–94.

Baumann, H.G., 1975. Merger theory, property rights, and the pattern of U.S. direct investment in Canada. Weltwirtshaftliches Archiv III, 676–698.

Beamish, P.W. & Inkpen, A., 1998. Japanese firms and the decline of the Japanese expatriate. *Journal of World Business,* 33(1), 35–50.

Berle, A. & Means, G., 1965. *The Modern Corporation and Private Property*. Macmillan, New York.

Bevan, A.A., & Estrin, S., 2004. The determinants of foreign direct investment into European transition economies. *Journal of Comparative Economics*, 32, 775–787.

Birkinshaw, J.M., & Morrison, A.J., 1995. Configurations of strategy and structure in subsidiaries of multinational corporations. *Journal of International Business Studies*, 26(4), 729–753.

Birkinshaw, J., 2001. Making sense of knowledge management. *Ivey Business Journal*, 65(4), 32–36.

Blair, M., 1995. Rethinking assumptions behind corporate governance. *Challenge*, Nov–Dec. (1995), 12–18.

Block, Z. & MacMillan, I., 1993. *Corporate Venturing*. Harvard Business Press, Cambridge, MA.

Blomstermo, A., Sharma, D.D., & Sallis, J. 2006. Choice of foreign market entry mode in service firms. *International Marketing Review*, 23(2), 211–22.

Boojihawon, D.K., Dimitratos, P., & Young, S., 2007. Characteristics and influences of multinational subsidiary entrepreneurial culture: The case of the advertising sector. *Journal of International Business Review*, 16(5), 549–572.

Bouquet, C., Hébert, L., & Delios, A., 2004. Foreign expansion in service industries: Reparability and human capital intensity. *Journal of Business Research*, 57(1), 35–46.

Branstetter, L., 2000. Is foreign investment a channel of knowledge spillovers? Evidence from Japan's FDI in the United States, NBER Working Paper 8015.

Brouthers, K.D., Brouthers, L.E., & Werner, S. 1996. Dunning's eclectic theory and the smaller firm: The impact of ownership and locational advantages on the choice of entry-modes in the computer software industry. *International Business Review*, 5(4), 377–394.

Brouthers, L.E., Brouthers, K.D., & Werner, S., 1999. Is Dunning's eclectic framework descriptive or normative? *Journal of International Business Studies*, 30, 831–844.

Brouthers, K. & Brouthers, L.E., 2002. Werner, S., Industrial sector, perceived environmental uncertainty and entry mode strategy. *Journal of Business Research*, 55(6): 495–507.

Brouthers, K.D. & Brouthers, L. E., 2001. Explaining the national culture distance paradox. *Journal of International Business Studies*, 32, 177–189.

Brouthers, K.D., 2002. Institutional, cultural and transaction costs influences on entry mode choice and performance. *Journal International Business Studies*, 33, 203–222.

Brouthers, L.E., Brouthers, K., & Werner, S., 2000. Perceived environmental uncertainty, entry mode choice and satisfaction with EC-MNC performance, *British Journal of Management*, 11, 183–195.

Brouthers, K.D. & Nakos, G. 2004. SME entry mode choice and performance: A transaction cost perspective. *Entrepreneurship: Theory and Practice*, 28(3), 229–247.

Brouthers, K.D., Brouthers, L.E., & Werner, S. 2008. Real options, international entry mode choice and performance. *Journal of Management Studies*, 45(5), 936–960.

Buckley, P. & Casson, M., 1976. *The Future of the Multinational Enterprise*. MacMillan Press, London.

Buckley, P.J. & Casson, M., 1996. An economic model of international joint venture strategy, *Journal of International Business Studies*, Special Issue, 849–876.

Buckley, P. & Casson, M., 1998. Models of the multinational enterprise. *Journal of International Business Studies* 29 2, pp. 21–44.

Buckley, P.J., & Casson M., 2000. Foreign market entry: A formal extension of internationalization theory, in Casson, M. (ed.), *Economics of International Business*. Edward Elgar, Chelthenham.

Buckley, P.J. & Carter, M.J., 2004. A formal analysis of knowledge combination in multinational enterprises. *Journal of International Business Studies*, 35, 371–384.

Burgel, O. & Murray, G.C. 2000. The international market entry choices of start-up companies in high-technology industries. *Journal of International Marketing*, 8(2) 33–62.

Castanias, R. & Helfat, C., 2001. The managerial rent model: Theory and empirical analysis. *Journal of Management*, 27(6), 661.

Caves, R.E. & Mehra, S.K., 1986. Entry of foreign multinational into U.S. manufacturing industries. In: Porter, M.E., Editor, *Competition in Global Industries*. Harvard Business School Press, Boston, MA, pp. 449–481.

Caves, R.E., 1971. International corporations: The industrial economics of foreign investment. *Economica*, 56, 279–293.

Caves, R., 1974. Multinational firms, competition, and productivity in host-country industries. *Economica*, 41, 176–193.

Caves, R.E., 1982. *Multinational Enterprise and Economic Analysis*. Cambridge University Press, Cambridge.

Caves, R.E., 1996. *Multinational Enterprise and Economic Analysis* (2nd ed.). Cambridge University Press, Cambridge, UK.

Cefis, E. & Marsili, O., 2006, Survivor: The role of innovation in firm's survival, *Research Policy*, 35, 621–641.

Chen, H. & Chen, T.J., 1998. Network linkages and location choice in foreign direct investment. *Journal of International Business Studies*, 29(3), 445–468.

Chen, J.R., & Yang C.H., 1999. Determinants of Taiwanese foreign direct investment—Comparison between expansionary FDI and defensive FDI. *Taiwan Economic Review*, 27(2), 215–240.

Chen, H. & Hu, Y.M., 2002. An analysis of determinants of entry mode and its impact on performance. *International Business Review*, 11(2), 193–210.

Chen, T. & Ku, Y., 2000. The effect of foreign direct investment on firm growth: The case of Taiwan's manufacturers. *Japan and the World Economy*, 12(2), 153–172.

Cheng, Y.-M. 2008. Asset specificity, experience, capability, host Government intervention, and ownership-based entry mode strategy for SMEs in International Markets. *International Journal of Commerce and Management*, 18(3), 207–233.

Chhibber, K.P. & Majumdar, K.S., 1999. Foreign ownership and profitability: Property rights, control, and the performance of firms in Indian industry. *The Journal of Law and Economics*, 42, 209–238.

Child, J., 1994. Management in China during the Age of Reform. *Cambridge University Press*, Cambridge, UK.

Child, J., Chung, L., & Davies, H., 2003. The performance of cross-border units in China: A test of natural selection, strategic choice and contingency theories. *Journal of International Business Studies*, 34, 242–254.

Cho, K.R., 1985. Multinational Banks: Their Identities and Determinants. *UMI Research Press*, Ann Arbor, MI.

Christman, D.D. & Yip, G.S., 1999. The relative influence of country conditions, industry structure, and business strategy on multinational corporation subsidiary performance. *Journal of International Management*, 5, 241–265.

Chung, W., 2001. Mode, size, and location of foreign direct investments and industry markup. *Journal of Economic Behavior & Organization*, 45(2), 185–211.

Coase, R., 1932. The nature of the firm. *Economica* 4, 386–405.Coase, R., 1937. The nature of the firm. *Economica*, 4(16), 386–405.

Crick, D. & Jones, M.V. 2000. Small high-technology firms and international high technology markets. *Journal of International Marketing*, 8(2), 63–85.

Csikszentmihalyi M., & Rochberg-Halton E., 1981. *The Meaning of Things: Domestic Symbols and the Self*. Cambridge University Press, Cambridge (Eng) New York.

Cubbin, J. & Geroski, P., 1987. The convergence of profits in the long run: Inter-firm and inter-industry comparisons. *Journal of Industrial Economics*. 35, pp. 427–441.

Culem, C.G., 1988. The locational determinants of direct investment among industrialized countries. *European Economic Review*, 32(2), 885–904

Cyert, R.D., & March, J.G., 1963. *A Behavioral Theory of the Firm*. Prentice Hall, Englewood Cliffs, NJ.

Das, S., 2002. Foreign direct investment and the relative wage in a developing economy. *Journal of Development Economics*, 67(1), 55–77.

Davidson, W.H., 1980. The location of foreign direct investment activity: Country characteristics and experience effects. *Journal of International Business Studies*, 11, 9–12.

Davis, P.S., Desai, A.B., & Francis, J.D. 2000. Mode of international entry: An isomorphism perspective. *Journal of International Business Studies*, 31, 239–258.

Davis, P., Desai, A.B., & Francis, J.D., 2002. Mode of international entry: An isomorphism perspective. *Journal of International Business Studies*, 31, 239–258.

Delios, A., & Beamish, P.W., 1999. Ownership strategy of Japanese firms: Transactional, institutional, and experience influences. *Strategic Management Journal*, 915–933.

Delios, A. & Beamish, P.W. 2001. Ownership strategy of Japanese firms: Transactional, institutional and experience influences. *Strategic Management Journal*, 20, 915–933.

Delios A. & Beamish P.W., 2001. Survival and profitability: The role of experience and intangible assets in foreign subsidiary performance. *Academy of Management Journal*, 44(5), 1028–1038.

Delios, A. & Beamish, P.W., 2004, Joint venture performance revisited: Japanese foreign subsidiaries worldwide. *Management International Review*, 44(1), 69–91.

Demirbag, M., Tatoglu, E., & Glaister, K.W., 2007, Factors influencing perceptions of performance: The case of western FDI in an emerging market. *International Business Review*, 16(3), 310–336.

Demirbag, M. & Mirza, H., 2000. Factors affecting international joint venture success: An empirical analysis of foreign-local partner relationships and performance in joint ventures in Turkey, *International Business Review*, 9(1), 1–35.

Dhawan, R., 2001. Firm size and productivity differential: theory and evidence from a panel of US firms. *Journal of Economic Behavior & Organization*, 44(3), 269–293.

Dierickx, I., & Cool, K., 1989. Asset stock accumulation and sustainability of competitive advantage. *Management Science*, 35(12), 1504–1513.

Dikova, D. & Witteloostuijn, A., 2007. Foreign direct investment mode choice: Entry and establishment modes in transition economies. *Journal of International Business Studies*, 38(6), 1013–1033.

Dunning, J.H., 1958. *American Investment in British Manufacturing Industry*. George Allen and Unwin, London.

Dunning, J.H., 1977. Trade, location of economic activity and the MNC: A search for an eclectic approach. In: Ohlin, B., Hesselborn, P.O., & Wijkman, P.M., Editors, *The International Allocation of Economic Activity*. Holmes and Meier, New York, pp. 395–418.

Dunning, J.H., 1979. Explaining Changing Patterns of International Production: In Defence of the Eclectic Theory. *Oxford Bulletin of Economics and Statistics*, 41, 269–295.

Dunning, J.H., 1980. Toward an eclectic theory of international production: Some empirical results. *Journal of International Business Studies*, 11 (Spring/Summer), 9–31.

Dunning, J.H., 1988. The eclectic paradigm of international production: A restatement and some possible extensions. *Journal of International Business Studies*, 26, 461–492.

Dunning, J.H., 1993. *Multinational Enterprise and the Global Economy*. Addison-Wesley Publishers, England.

Dunning, J.H., 1995. Reappraising the eclectic paradigm in an age of alliance capitalism. *Journal of International Business Studies*, 26, 461–491.

Dörrenbächer, C.H. & Gammelgaard, J., 2006. Subsidiary role development: The effect of micro-political headquarters subsidiary negotiations on the product, market and value-added scope of foreign-owned subsidiaries. *Journal of International Management*, 12(3), 266–283.

Elango, B. & Sambharya, R., 2004. The influence of industry structure on the entry mode choice of overseas entrants in manufacturing industries. *Journal of International Management*, 10(1), 107–124.

Eaton, J., & Tamura, A., 1996. Japanese and US Exports and Investment as Conduits of Growth, NBER Working Paper 5457.

Eicher, T., & Kang, J.W., 2005. Trade, foreign direct investment or acquisition: Optimal entry modes for multinationals. *Journal of Development Economics*, 77(1), 207–228.

Elschen, R., 1991. Shareholder Value und Agency-Theorie–Anreiz-und Kontrollsysteme für Zielsetzungen der Anteilseigner. *Betriebswirtschaftliche Forschung und Praxis*, 43(3), 209–220.

Erramilli, M.K., Agarwal, S., & Kim, S., 1997. Are firm-specific advantages location-specific too? *Journal of International Business Studies*. 28, 735–757.

Erramilli, M.K. 1989. Entry mode choice in service industries. *International Marketing Review*, 7(5), 50–62

Erramilli, M.K. 1992. Influence of some external and internal environmental factors on foreign market entry mode choice in service firms. *Journal of Business Research*, 25(4), 263–276.

Erramilli, M.K. & Rao, C.P. 1993. Service firms' international entry-mode choice: A modified transaction-cost analysis approach. *The Journal of Marketing*, 57(3), 19–38.

Erramilli, M.K. & D'Souza, D.E. 1993. Venturing into foreign markets: The case of the small service firm. *Entrepreneurship: Theory and Practice*, 17(4), 29–41.

Erramilli, M.K., Agarwal, S., & Dev, C.S. 2002. Choice between non-equity entry modes: An organizational capability perspective. *Journal of International Business Studies*, 33, 223–242.

Fernández, Z. & Nieto, M.J. 2006. Impact of ownership on the international involvement of SMEs. *Journal of International Business Studies*, 37(3), 340–351.

Fligstein, N. & Freeland, R., 1995. Theoretical and comparative perspectives on corporate organization. *Annual Review of Sociology*, 21(1995), 21–44.

Flowers, E., 1976. Oligopolistic reaction in European and Canadian direct investment in the United States. *Journal of International Business Studies*, 7, 43–55.

Foss, N.J. & Pedersen, T., 2002. Transferring knowledge in MNCs: The role of sources of subsidiaries knowledge and organizational context. *Journal of International Management*, 8, 49–67.

Forsgren, M., 1989. *Managing the Internationalization Process — The Swedish Case*. Routledge, London.

Forsgren, M., 2008. *Theories of the Multinational Firm: A Multidimensional Creature in the Global Economy*. Edward Elgar, Cheltenham, UK.

Forsyth, D.C.J., 1972. *US Investment in Scotland. Praeger Special Studies in International Economics and Development*. Praeger, New York.

Froot, K.A., & Stein, J.C., 1991. Exchange rates and foreign direct investment: An imperfect capital markets approach. *The Quarterly Journal of Economics*, 106(4), 1191–1217.

Frost, T.S., 2001. The geographic sources of foreign subsidiaries' innovations. *Strategic Management Journal*, 22(2), 101–123.

Geringer, M. & Hebert, L., 1991. Measuring performance of international joint ventures. *Journal of International Business Studies*, 22(2), 249–263.

Glaister, K.W. & Buckley, P.J., 1999. Performance relationships in UK international alliances. *Management International Review*, 39(2), 123–147.

Goldberg, M.A., 1972. The determinants of US Direct Investment in the EEC: Comment. *The American Economic Review*, 62(4), 692–699.

Gomes-Casseres, B. 1990. Firm ownership preferences and host government restrictions: An integrated approach. *Journal of International Business Studies*, 21(1), 1–22.

Gomes, L., & Ramaswamy, K., 1999. An empirical examination of the form of the relationship between multinationality and performance. *Journal of International Business Studies*, 30, 173–188.

Graham, E., 1978. Transatlantic investment by multinational business firms: A rivalistic phenomenon, *Journal of Post Keynesian Economics*, 1, 82–99.

Graham, E.M., & Krugman, P.R., 1991. Foreign Direct Investment in the United States. *Institute for International Economics*, Washington, DC.

Grant, R.M., 1991. The resource-based theory of competitive advantage: Implications for strategy formulation. *California Management Review*, 33(3), 114–135.

Gruber, W., Mehta D., & Vernon E., 1967. The research and development factor in investment of U.S. industries. *Journal of Political Economy*, 75, 20–37.

Gupta, A. & Govindarajan, V., 2000. Knowledge flows within multinational corporations. *Strategic Management Journal*, 21, 473–496.

Gupta, S., Clements, B., Baldacci, E., & Mulas-Granados, C., 2002. Expenditure Composition, Fiscal Adjustment, and Growth in Low-income Countries, IMF Working Paper No. 02/77.

Hadley, R.D. & Wilson, H.I.M., 2003. The network model of internationalization and experiential knowledge. *International Business Review*, 12, 697–717.

Hair, J., Anderson, R.E., Tatham, R.L., & Black, W.C., 1995. *Multivariate Data Analysis with Readings.* Prentice-Hall, Englewood Cliffs, NJ.

Hanel, P., 2000. R&D, inter-industry and international technology spillovers and the total factor productivity growth of manufacturing industries in Canada, 1974–1989. *Economic Systems Research,* 12(3), 345–361.

Hannon, J., Huang, I., & Jaw, B., 1995. International human resource strategy and its determinants: The case of subsidiaries in Taiwan. *Journal of International Business Studies,* 26(3), 531–554.

Harrigan, K.R., 1981. Barriers to entry and competitive strategy. *Strategic Management Journal.* 2, 395–412.

Hastings, M., 1999. A new operational paradigm for oil operations in sensitive environments: An analysis of social pressure, corporate capabilities and competitive advantage. *Business Strategy and the Environment,* 8, 267–280.

Hartman, D., 1985. Tax policy and foreign direct investment. *Journal of Public Economics,* 26(1), 107–121.

Harzing, A.W., 2002. Acquisitions vs. greenfields: International strategy and management of entry modes. *Strategic Management Journal,* 23, 211–227.

Hawawini, G., Subramanian, V., & Verdin, P., 2003. Is performance driven by industry- or firm-specific factors? A new look at the evidence. *Strategic Management Journal,* 24 (2003), pp. 1–16.

Hennart, J., 1989. Can the "new forms of investment" substitute for the "old forms?" A transactions cost perspective. *Journal of International Business Studies,* 20, 211–234.

Hennart, J.F., Kim D.J., & Zeng, M., 1998. The impact of joint venture status on the longevity of Japanese stakes in U.S. manufacturing affiliates. *Organization Science,* 9(3), 382–395.

Hennart, J.F. & Larimo, J., 1997. The impact of culture on the strategy of multinational enterprises: Does national origin affect ownership decision? *Journal of International Business Studies,* 29, 515–538.

Hennart, J.F. & Reddy, S., 1997. The choice between mergers/acquisitions and joint ventures: The case of Japanese investors in the United States. *Strategic Management Journal,* 18, 1–12.

Hennart, J.F. & Park, Y.R., 1993. Greenfield vs. acquisition: The strategy of Japanese investors in the United States. *Management Science,* 39(9), 1054–1070.

Herrmann, P. & Datta, D.K. 2005. Relationships between top management team characteristics and international diversification: An empirical investigation*. *British Journal of Management,* 16, 69–78.

Hirsch, S., 1967. *Location of Industry and International Competitiveness.* Oxford University Press.

Horaguchi, H. & Toyne, B., 1990. Setting the record straight: Hymer, internationalization theory and transaction cost economics. *Journal of International Business Studies*, 21, 487–494.

Hoskisson, R.E., & Busenitz, W. 2002 Market uncertainty and learning distance. In corporate entrepreneurship entry mode choice. In. Hitt, M.A., Ireland, R.D., Camp, S.M., & Sexton D.L. (Eds.), *Strategic Entrepreneurship: Creating a New Mindset* (pp. 151–172). Blackwell Publishing, Oxford.

Hymer, S.H., 1966. Direct foreign investment and the national interest. In Russell P. (Ed.), *Nationalism in Canada*. McGraw-Hill, Toronto.

Hymer, S.H., 1976. *The International Operations of National Firms: A Study of Foreign Direct Investment*. MIT Press, Cambridge, MA.

Ito, K. & Fukao, K., 2005. Foreign direct investment and trade in Japan: An empirical analysis based on the establishment and enterprise census for 1996. *Journal of the Japanese and International Economies*, 19, 414–445.

Jemison, D.B. & Sitkin, S.B., 1986. Corporate acquisitions: A process perspective. *The Academy of Management Review*, 11(1), 145–163.

Jensen, R. & Szulanski, G., 2004. Stickiness and the adaptation of organizational practices in cross-border knowledge transfer. *Journal of International Business Studies*, 35, 508–523.

Johanson, J. & Vahlne, J.E., 1977. The internationalization process of the firm: A model of knowledge development and increasing foreign market commitments. *Journal of International Business Studies*, 81, 23–32.

Kim, K., Lee, S.H., & Rhee, G., 2007. Large shareholder monitoring and regulation: The Japanese banking experience. *Journal of Economics and Business*, 59(5), 466–486.

Kimura, F., 1989. Heat flux on mixture of different land-use surface: Test of a new parameterization scheme. *Journal of the Meteorological Society of Japan*, 67, 401–409.

Kimura, Y., 1989. Firm-specific strategic advantages and foreign direct investment behavior of firms: The case of Japanese semiconductor firms. *Journal of International Business Studies*, 20(2), 296–314.

Kimura, Y., & Pugel, T.A., 1995. Keiretsu and Japanese direct investment in US manufacturing. *Japan and the World Economy*, 7(4), 481–503.

Kindleberger, C.P., 1969. *American Business Abroad: Six Lectures on Direct Investment*. Yale University Press, New Haven and London:.

Kiyota, K. & Urata, S., 2007. The Role of Multinational Firms in International Trade: The Case of Japan, working papers 560. Research Seminar in International Economics, University of Michigan.

Knickerbocker, F.T., 1973. *Oligopolistic Reaction and Multinational Enterprise*. Harvard University, Boston.

Kogut, B. & Zander, U., 1993. Knowledge of the firm and the evolutionary theory of the multinational corporation. *Journal of International Business Studies*, 244, 625–645.

Kogut, B., 1989. The stability of joint ventures: Reciprocity and competitive rivalry. *Journal of Industrial Economics*, 38(2), 183–198.

Kogut, B. & Singh, H., 1988. The effect of national culture on the choice of entry mode. *Journal of International Business Studies*, 19, 411–432.

Kokko, A., Zejan, M., & Tansini, R., 2001. Trade regimes and spillover effects of FDI: Evidence from Uruguay. *Weltwirtschaftliches Archiv*, 137, 124–149.

Kostova, T., 1999. Transnational transfer of strategic organizational practices: A contextual perspective. *Academy of Management Review*, 24(2), 308–324.

Krugman, P. & Venables, A., Editors, 1994. *The Location of Economic Activity: New Theories and Evidence*. Center of Economic Policy Research, London.

Kumar, N., 1996. The power of trust in manufacturer-retailer relationships. *Harvard Business Review*, 74(6), 92.

Kwon, Y.-C. & Konopa, L.J., 1992, Impact of host country market characteristics on the choice of foreign market entry mode. *International Marketing Review*, 10, 60–76.

Lall, S., & Streeten, P., 1977. *Foreign Investment, Transnationals and Developing Countries*. Macmillan, London.

Lall, S., 1980. Monopolistic advantages and foreign involvement by US manufacturing industry. *Oxford Economic Papers*, 32, 102–122.

Lang, L.H.P., & Ofek, E., 1995. Why do firms invest in Eastern Europe? *European Financial Management*, 1, 147–171.

Larimo, J., 1994. Foreign direct investments behavior and performance of Finnish firms in EC countries, *Proceedings of the University of Vaasa*, Discussion Papers 178.

Lee, G., 2006. The effectiveness of international knowledge spillover channels. *European Economic Review*, 50(8), 2075–2088.

Li, J. & Guisinger, S., 1991. How well do foreign firms compete in the United States? *Business Horizons*, 34(6), 49–53.

Li, J., 1995. Foreign entry and survival: Effects of strategic choices on performance in international market. *Strategic Management Journal*, 16, 333–351.

Li, L. & Qian, G., 2008. Partnership or self-reliance entry modes: Large and small technology-based enterprises' strategies in overseas markets. *Journal of International Entrepreneurship*, 6(4), 188–208.

Lipsey, R.E., 1999. *Foreign production by US firms and parent firm employment* (No. w7357). National Bureau of Economic Research.

Liu, Y.P., 2017. Born global firms' growth and collaborative entry mode: the role of transnational entrepreneurs. *International Marketing Review*, 34(1), 46–67.

Lu, J., & Beamish, P.W., 2001. The Internationalization and Performance of SMEs. *Strategic Management Journal*, 22(6), 565–586.

Lu, J.W. & Beamish, P.W. 2006. SME internationalization and performance: Growth vs. profitability. *Journal of international entrepreneurship*, 4(1), 27–48.

Lu, J.W., 2002. Intra- and inter-organizational imitative behavior: Institutional influences on Japanese firms' entry mode choice. *Journal of International Business Studies*, 33(1), 19–37.

Lu, J.W & Hebert, L., 2005. Equity control and the survival of international joint ventures. *Journal of Business Research*, 58(6), 736–745.

Luo, Y., 2001. Determinants of entry in an emerging economy: A multilevel approach. *Journal of Management Studies*, 38(3), 443–472.

Luo, Y., 1996. Evaluating the performance of strategic alliances in China. *Long Range Planning*, 29(4), 534–542.

Luo, Y., & Peng, M.W., 1999. Learning to compete in a transition economy: Experience, environment and performance. *Journal of International Business Studies*, 30(2), 269–296.

Luo, Y. & Tan, J.J., 1997. How much does industry structure impact foreign direct investment in China? *International Business Review*, 6(4), 337–359.

Madhok, A., 1997. Cost, value and foreign market entry mode: The transaction and the firm. *Strategic Management Journal*, 18(1): 39–61.

Maekelburger, B., Schwens, C., & Kabst, R. 2012. Asset specificity and foreign market entry mode choice of small and medium-sized enterprises: The moderating influence of knowledge safeguards and institutional safeguards. *Journal of International Business Studies*, 43(5), 458–476.

Mahoney, J.T. & Pandian, J.R. 1992. The resource-based view within the conversation of strategic management. *Strategic Management Journal*, 13 (5) 363–380.

Makino, S., & Beamish, P. W., 1998. Performance and survival of joint ventures with non-conventional ownership structures. *Journal of International Business Studies*, 29(4), 797–818.

Makino, S., & Delios, A., 1996. Local knowledge transfer and performance: Implications for alliance formation in Asia, *Journal of International Business Studies*, 27, 905–927.

Makino, S., Beamish, P.W., & Zhao, M.B., 2004. The characteristics and performance of Japanese FDI in less developed and developed countries. *Journal of World Business*, 39(4), 377–392.

Mansfield, E., Romeo, A., & Wagner, S., 1979. Foreign trade and US research and development. *Review of Economics and Statistics*, 61, 49–57.

Mansour, M. & Hoshino Y., 2002. Entry mode choice of the Japanese MNCs in Europe: Impact of firm and industrial factors. *Japanese Journal of Administrative Science*, 15(3), 231–247.

March, J.G., 1991. Exploration and exploitation in organizational learning. *Organization Science*, 2(1), 71–87.

Markusen, J. R., & Venables, A. J., 1999. Foreign direct investment as a catalyst for industrial development. *European Economic Review*, 43(2), 335–356.

McManus, J., 1972. The theory of international firm. In Paguet, G. (Ed.), *The Multinational Firm and the Nation State*. Collier, Toronto, Canada.

Melville, I., 1999. *Marketing in Japan*. Butterworth-Heinemann, Woburn.

Meyer, J.W., & Rowan, B., 1977. Institutionalized organizations: Formal structure as myth and ceremony. *American Journal of Sociology*, 83(2), 340–363.

Meyer, K.E., 1998. *Direct Investment in Economies in Transition*. Edward Elgar, Aldershot.

Meyer, K.E., & Nguyen, H.V. 2005. Foreign investment strategies and sub-national institutions in emerging markets: Evidence from Vietnam. *Journal of Management Studies*, 42, 63–93.

Moore, M.O., 1993. Determinants of German manufacturing direct investment in manufacturing industries. *Weltwirtschaftliches Archiv*, 129, 120–137.

Moosa, I.A., 2002. *Foreign Direct Investment: Theory, Evidence and Practice*. Palgrave, London.

Morschett, D., 2007. *Institutionalization and Coordination of Foreign Affiliates: Analysis of Manufacturing and Service industries*. Gabler, Wiesbaden.

Morschett, D., Schramm-Klein, H., & Zentes, J., 2015. *Strategic International Management, Text and Cases*. Springer Gabler, Berlin.

Mudambi, R., 2002. The location decision of the multinational firm: A survey. In McCann P., (ed.), *Industrial Location Economics*. Edward Elgar, Cheltenham.

Mutinelli, M. & Piscitello, L., 1998. The entry mode choice of MNCs: An evolutionary approach, *Research Policy*, 27(5), 491–506.

Nakos, G. & Brouthers, K.D. 2002. Entry mode choice of SMEs in central and eastern Europe. *Entrepreneurship: Theory and Practice*, 27(1), 47–63.

Nelson, R.R., & Winter, S.G., 1982. *An Evolutionary Theory of Economic Change*. Harvard University Press, Cambridge, MA.

Nitsch, D., Beamish, P. W. & Makino, S.H., 1995. Characteristics and performance of Japanese foreign direct investment in Europe. *European Management Journal*, 13(3), 276–285.

Nitsch, D., Beamish, P.W., & Makino, S., 1996. Entry mode and performance of Japanese FDI in Western Europe. *Management International Review*, 36(1), 27–44.

Nohria, N., Ghoshal, S., 1994. Differentiated fit and shared values: Alternatives for managing headquarters-subsidy relations. *Journal of Management and Strategy*, 15(6), 491–502.

Nohria, N., & Ghoshal, S., 1997. *The Differentiated Network: Organizing Multinational Corporations for Value Creation*. Jossey-Bass Publishers, San Francisco, CA.

OECD, 2002. Foreign Direct Investment for Development: Maximizing Benefits and Minimizing Costs, Organization for Economic Cooperation and Development (OECD).

OECD, 2007. International Investment Perspectives: Freedom of Investment in a Changing World, Organization for Economic Cooperation and Development (OECD).

Ogasavara, M.H. & Hoshino, Y., 2007a, The impact of ownership, internalization, and entry mode on Japanese subsidiaries' performance in Brazil. *Japan and the World Economy*, 19(1), 1–25.

Ogasavara, M. H., & Hoshino, Y., 2007b. An investigation of the effects of international entry strategies for firm survival: Evidence from Japanese manufacturing firms in Brazil. Working paper, University of Tsukuba.

Ojala, A. & Tyrväinen, P. 2006. Business models and market entry mode choice of small software firms. *Journal of International Entrepreneurship*, 4(2–3), 69–81.

Oliver, C. 1997. Sustainable competitive advantage: Combining institutional and resource-based views. *Strategic Management Journal*, 18(9), 697–713.

Pak, O.S. and Park, Y.R., 2005. Characteristics of Japanese FDI in the East and the West: Understanding the strategic motives of Japanese investment. *Journal of World Business*, 40(3), 254–266.

Pan, Y. & Tse, D., 2000. The hierarchical model of market entry modes. *Journal of International Business Studies*, 31, 535–554.

Pan, Y., & Chi, P., 1999. Financial performance and survival of multinational corporations in China. *Strategic Management Journal*, 20(4), 359–374.

Pan, Y., Li, S., & Chi, P.S.K., 1999. The impact of order and mode of market entry on profitability and market share. *Journal of International Business Studies*, 30, 80–101.

Pangarkar, N. & Lim, H., 2003. Performance of foreign direct investment from Singapore. *International Business Review*, 12(5), 601–624.

Parker G.A., 1974. Assessment strategy and the evolution of fighting behaviour. *Journal of Theoretical Biology*, 47, 223–243.

Parthasarathy, B. & Aoyama, Y., 2006. From software services to R&D services: Local entrepreneurship in the software industry in Bangalore, India. *Journal of Environment and Planning*, 38(7), 1269–1285.

Paul, D.L., & Wooster, R.B., 2008. Strategic investments by US firms in transition economies. *Journal of International Business Studies*, 39(2), 249–266.

Pedersen, T. & Petersen, B., 1998. Explaining gradually increasing resource commitment to a foreign market, *International Business Review*, 75, pp. 483–501.

Peteraf, M.A., 1993. The cornerstones of competitive advantage: A resource-based view. *Strategic Management Journal*, 14(2), 179–191.

Petrochilos G., 1989. *Foreign Direct Investment and the Development Process*: *The Case of Greece*. Lanchester Polytechnic, UK.

Pierce, J., Kostova, T., & Dirks, K., 2001. Toward a theory of psychological ownership in organizations. *The Academy of Management Review*, 26(2), 298–310.

Pinho, J.C. 2007. The impact of ownership: Location-specific advantages and managerial characteristics on SME foreign entry mode choices. *International Marketing Review*, 24(6), 715–734.

Porter, M.E., 1980. *Competitive Advantage*. Free press, New York.

Pothukuchi, V., Damanpour, F., Choi, J., Chen C.C., & Park, SH., 2002. National and organizational culture differences and international joint venture performance. *Journal of International Business Studies*, 33(2), 243–265.

Pradeep K., & Chhibber, K., 1999. Foreign ownership rules and domestic firm globalization in India. Working paper, University of California, Berkeley.

Prashantham, S. 2011. Social capital and Indian micro multinationals. *British Journal of Management*, 22(1), 4–20.

Radner, R., 1992. Hierarchy: The economics of managing. *Journal of Economic Literature*, 30, 1382–1415.

Ramaswamy, K., Gomes, L., & Veliyath, R., 1998. The performance correlates of ownership control: A study of U.S. and European MNC joint ventures in India. *International Business Review*, 7(4), 423–441.

Rasheed, H.S. 2005. Foreign entry mode and performance: The moderating effects of environment. *Journal of Small Business Management*, 43(1), 41–54.

Rasiah, R., 2003. Foreign ownership, technology and electronics exports from Malaysia and Thailand. *Journal of Asian Economics*, 14(5), 785–811.

Rasouli Ghahroudi, M., Turnbull, S. J., & Hoshino, Y., 2010. Assets growth, foreign ownership and type of industry in multinational companies. *International Business Research*, 3(4), 244–255.

Rasouli Ghahroudi, M., & Hoshino, Y., 2007. Establishment, survival, sales growth and entry strategies of Japanese MNCs subsidiaries in India. *Journal of Developmental Entrepreneurship*, 12(4), 433–447.

Rasouli Ghahroudi, M., 2011. Ownership advantages and firm factors influencing performance of foreign affiliates in Japan, *International Journal of Business and Management*, 6(11), 119–137.

Razin, A., Sadka, E., & Yuen, C.W., 1999. *Excessive FDI flows under asymmetric information* (No. w7400). National bureau of economic research.

Reed, R. & DeFillippi, R.J., 1990. Causal ambiguity, barrier to imitation, and sustainable competitive advantage. *Academy of Management Review*, 15, 88–102.

Reuber, A.R. & Fischer, E. 1997. The influence of the management team's international experience on the internationalization behaviors of SMEs. *Journal of International Business Studies*, 28, 807–825.

Richter, R., & Furubotn, E., 2003. *Neue Institutionenökonomik: Eine Einführung und kritische Würdigung*, 3. Auflage. Mohr Siebeck, Tübingen.

Riedel, J., 1975. The nature and determinants of exported oriented foreign investment in a developing country: A case study of Taiwan. *Weltwirtsch Arch* 3(3), 505–528.

Rihai-Belkaoui, A., 1998. The effects of the degree of internationalization on firm performance. *International Business Review*, 7(3), 315–321.

Ripolles Meliá, M., Blesa Pérez, A., & Roig Dobón, S. 2010. The influence of innovation orientation on the internationalization of SMEs in the service sector. *The Service Industries Journal*, 30(5), 777–791.

Ripollés, M., Blesa, A., & Monferrer, D. 2012. Factors enhancing the choice of higher resource commitment entry modes in international new ventures. *International Business Review*, 21(4), 648–666.

Roberto, B. 2004. Acquisition versus greenfield investment: The location of foreign manufacturers in Italy. *Regional Science and Urban Economics*, 34, 3–25.

Roquebert, J.A., Phillips, R.L., & Westfall, P.A., 1996. Market vs. management: What drives profitability? *Strategic Management Journal*, 17, pp. 653–664.

Saffu, K., & Manu, T., 2004. Strategic capabilities of Ghanaian female business owners and the performance of their ventures, working paper, Brock University, Ontario.

Saunders, R., 1983. The determinants of interindusty variation of foreign ownership in Canadian manufacturing. *Canadian Journal of Economics*, 15, 77–84.

Schaefer Axel, O., 2002. Market entry and organizational form", For the seminar: "Theories and Concepts of Internationalization and FDI" Summer Term, Faculty of Economics, Professorship for Organization and International Management, the University of Paderborn.

Scherer, F.M., 1980. *Industrial Market Structure and Economic Performance*. Rand McNally, Chicago.

Schlegelmilch, B.B. & Chini, T.C., 2003. Knowledge transfer between marketing functions in multinational companies: A conceptual model. *International Business Review*, 12, 215–232.

Schmalensee, R., 1989. Inter-industry studies of structure and performance. In: Schmalensee, R. & Willing, R., Editors, *Handbook of Industrial Organization,* Vol. II. Elsevier, New York, pp. 952–1009.

Schneider, F., & Frey, B.S., 1985. Economic and political determinants of foreign direct investment. *World Development*, 13(2), 161–175.

Schwens, C., Eiche, J., & Kabst, R. 2011. The moderating impact of informal institutional distance and formal institutional risk on SME entry mode choice. *Journal of Management Studies*, 48(2), 330–351.

Sengupta, P., 1998. Corporate disclosure quality and the cost of debt. *The Accounting Review*, 73(4), 459–474.

Sharma K., 2000. Export Growth in India- has FDI Played a Role? Yale University Discussion Paper No. 816.

Sharma, K., 2003. Factors determining India's export performance. *Journal of Asian Economics*, 14(3), 435–446.

Shi, Y.Z., Ho, P.Y., & Siu, W.S. 2001. Market entry mode selection: The experience of small firms in Hong Kong investing in China. *Asia Pacific Business Review*, 8(1) 19–41.

Shrader, J.M., 2001. Collaboration and performance in foreign markets: The case of young high-technology firms. *Academic Management Journal*, 44, 45–60.

Sing, H., & Jun, K.W., 1995. *Some New Evidence on Determinants of Foreign Direct Investment in Developing Countries*. Policy Research Working Paper 1531, World Bank, Washington DC.

Singh, K., 2005. Foreign direct investment in India: A critical analysis of FDI from 1991–2005, discussion paper, Center for Civil Society, New Delhi.

Sinha, U., 2005. International joint venture: Buy-out and subsidiary. *Journal of Economic Behavior & Organization.* Elsevier, doi: 10.1016/j.jebo.2005.10.004, 65, 734–756.

Siripaisalpipat, P. & Hoshino, Y., 2000. Firm-specific advantages, entry modes, and performance of Japanese FDI in Thailand, *Japan and the World Economy*, 12(1), 33–48.

Somlev, I.P., & Hoshino, Y., 2005. Influence of location factors on establishment and ownership of foreign investments: The case of the Japanese manufacturing firms in Europe. *International Business Review*, 14, 577–598.

Srinivasan, T.N., 1998. India's export performance: A comparative analysis, In I. J. Ahluwalia & I.M.D. Little (Eds.). *India's Economic Reforms and Development: Essay for Manmohan Singh.* Oxford University Press, Delhi.

Sudarsanam, P.S., 2003. *Creating Value from Mergers and Acquisitions.* Pearson Education, Harlow, Essex.

Svensson, R., 1996. Effects of overseas production on home country exports: Evidence based on Swedish multinationals. *Weltwirtschaftliches Archiv*, 132(2), 304–329.

Swoboda, B., 2002. *Dynamic Processes of Internationalization: Management Theories and Empirical Perspectives of Entrepreneurial Change.* Gabler, Wiesbaden.

Tatoglu, E. & Glaister, K.W., 1998. Performance of international joint ventures in Turkey: Perspectives of Western firms and Turkish firms, International Business Review, 7, 635–656.

Teece, D.J., 1976. *The Multinational Corporation and the Resource Cost of International Technology Transfer.* Ballinger, Cambridge, MA.

Teece, D.J., 1977. Technology transfer by multinational firms: The resource cost of transferring technological know-how. *The Economic Journal*, 87, 242–261.

Tihanyi L., Griffith, D.A., & Russell, C.J., 2005. The effect of cultural distance on entry mode Choice, international diversification, and MNE performance: A meta-analysis. *Journal of International Business Studies*, 36(3), 270–283.

Toyo Keizai Inc., 2001–2006. Toyo Keizai Databank, Kaigai Shinsutsu Kigyou Souran (Japanese Overseas Investments): listed by countries. Toyo Keizai Inc., Tokyo.

Trevino, L., & Grosse, R., 2002. An analysis of firm-specific resources and foreign direct investment in the United States, *International Business Review*, 11(4), 431–452.

Tschoegl, A., 2000. Entry and survival: The case of foreign banks in Norway. *Scandinavian Journal of Management*, 18(2), 131–153.

Turner, P.P., 1980. Import competition and the profitability of United Kingdom manufacturing industry. *Journal of Industrial Economics*, 29, 155–165.

Uhlenbruck, K., 2004. Developing acquired foreign subsidiaries: The experience of MNCs in transition economies. *Journal of International Business Studies*, 35(2), 109–123.

UNCTAD, 1999. *World Investment Report: Foreign Direct Investment and the Challenge of Development.* New York and Geneva, United Nations.

Vaupel, J.W., 1971. Characteristics and motivations of the US corporations which manufacture abroad. In *Meeting of Participating Members of the Atlantic Institute, Paris, June.*

Vega-Cespedes, C. & Hoshino, Y., 2002. Effects of ownership, and internalization advantages on performance: A comparative study of Japanese manufacturing and service subsidiaries in the United States and Latin America. *Japanese Journal of Administrative Science*, 16(2), 163–177.

Vermeulen, F. & Barkema, H., 2001. Learning through acquisitions. *Academy of Management Journal*, 44(3), 457–476.

Vernon, R., 1966. International investment and international trade in the product cycle. *Quarterly Journal of Economics*, 80, 190–207.

Vernon, R., 1971. Sovereignty at bay: The multinational spread of US enterprises. *The International Executive*, 13(4), 1–3.

Vernon, R., 1974. The location of economic activity, in Dunning, J.H., (ed.), *Economic Analysis and Multinational Enterprise*. Allen and Unwin, London.

Welch, L.S., Benito, G.R.G., & Petersen, B., 2007. *Foreign Operation Methods*: *Theory*, *Analysis*, *Strategy*. Edward Elgar, Cheltenham.

Wernerfelt, B., 1984. A resource-based view of the firm. *Strategic Management Journal*, 5, 171–180.

Wheeler, D., &. Mody, A., 1990. *Risk and Rewards in International Location Tournaments*: *The Case of US Firms*. The World Bank, Washington DC.

Williamson, O., 1985. *The Economic Institutions of Capitalism*. The Free Press, New York.

Wilson, B.D., 1980. *Disinvestment of Foreign Subsidiaries*. UMI, Ann Arbor, MI.

Woodcock, C.P., Beamish, P.W., & Makino, S., 1994. Ownership-based entry mode strategies and international performance. *Journal of International Business Studies*, 25, 253–273.

Woratschek, H., & Roth, S., 2005. Kooperation: Erklärungsperspektive der Neuen Institutionenökonomik. In ZENTES, J.; SWOBODA, B.; MORSCHETT, D. (Eds.): Kooperationen, Allianzen und Netzwerke, 2nd ed., Wiesbaden, Gabler, pp. 141–166.

Yang, J.Y.Y., Groenewold, N., & Tcha, M., 2000. The determinants of foreign direct investment in Australia. *Economic Record*, 76, 45–54.

Yeniyurt, S., Cavusgil, S.T., & Hult, G.T.M., 2005, A global market advantage framework: The role of global market knowledge competencies. *International Business Review*, 14, 1–19.

Yiu, D. & Makino, S. 2002. The choice between joint venture and wholly owned subsidiary: An institutional perspective. *Organization Science*, 13, 667–683.

Yoshida, M., 2004. Expanding Japanese presence in East Asia reflects shift to offshore production, JETRO Working Paper #1, Japanese External Trade Office, Tokyo.

Yu, C. & Ito, K., 1988. Oligopolistic reaction and foreign direct investment: The case of the U.S. tire and textiles industries. *Journal of International Business Studies*, 19(3), 449–460.

Zahra, S.A, 1991. Predictors and financial outcomes of corporate entrepreneurship: An exploratory study. *Journal of Business Venturing*, 6(4), 259–285.

Zahra, A., Ireland, R.D., & Hitt, M.A., 2000. International expansion by new venture firms: International diversity, mode of market entry, technological learning, and performance. *Academy of Management Journal*, 43(5), 925–950.

Zahra, S.A. & Hayton, J.C., 2008. The effect of international venturing on firm performance: The moderating influence of absorptive capacity. *Journal of Business Venturing*, 23(2), 195–220.

Zain, M. & Ng, S.I. 2006. The impacts of network relationships on SMEs' internationalization process. *Thunderbird International Business Review*, 48(2), 183–205.

Zejan, M.C., 1990. New ventures or acquisitions. The choice of Swedish multinational enterprises. *The Journal of Industrial Economics*, 38(3), 349–355.

# Index

accountability, 138
administrative, 5, 70
administratively, 22
advantages, 13, 17
ambivalent, 3

borrowing, 3

colonialism, 2
commitments, 13, 31, 50, 71, 73, 77, 103, 111, 138
competitiveness, 10, 77, 139
cultural distance, 45, 97, 107, 111, 113, 128, 138

disadvantages, 12, 46, 106, 112
discrimination, 8, 67
domestic, 3
domestic firms, 5, 6, 45, 78
domestic market, 4, 10, 49, 139

employment, 3, 12, 30, 85, 86, 118, 127, 134, 137

entry mode, 14, 23–25, 28, 29, 45, 52, 54, 64, 68, 69, 73–76, 84, 103, 105, 107–110, 113
entry strategy, 46, 52, 54, 58, 62, 65, 72, 87, 110, 134
equity ownership, 1, 8, 11, 45, 46, 50–53, 55–57, 61, 62, 64–66, 68, 69, 77, 78, 80, 84, 97, 100, 102, 104, 109, 111, 114, 115, 132–136, 139
export orientation, 10, 64, 139
export ratios, 9, 78, 86, 93, 100, 103, 106, 118, 126, 132

factor endowment, 10, 22, 139
financing, 3, 21
firm-specific, 18, 68, 84
firm-specific advantages, 3, 4, 12, 105, 107, 114, 119
firm specific factors, 9, 12, 64, 72, 105, 118, 132
foreign affiliates, 1, 5, 7, 47, 51, 65, 67, 72, 78, 80, 82, 84, 85, 94, 96,

102–104, 114, 115, 118, 123,
126–129, 131–135, 137, 139
foreign company, 2
Foreign direct investment, 1
foreign firms, 8, 16, 20, 39, 45, 52,
67, 77, 106, 108, 110, 112, 114, 119
foreign manager, 8, 68, 69, 72, 80,
82, 84, 85, 93, 96, 97, 103, 104,
118, 123, 132, 133, 135, 139
foreign managership, 80
foreign markets, 7, 18, 22, 31, 46, 51,
68, 76, 109, 111, 113, 127, 133
foreign ownership, 2, 3, 8, 9, 46, 49,
58, 67, 68, 71, 77, 84, 93, 96, 100,
102–104, 106, 114, 126, 128, 131,
132, 136, 137
foreign subsidiary, 2, 7, 16, 26, 32,
51, 64, 65, 68, 73
franchising, 2, 22

host country, 1–9, 12, 14–16, 21–24,
32, 45, 49, 50, 52, 64, 65, 68, 69,
73, 75, 85, 86, 93, 97, 103, 106–
109, 111–114, 117, 128,
134–136, 138
host market, 6–10, 24, 75, 85, 109,
123, 126–128, 131, 132, 136, 137,
139
human capital, 9, 10, 13, 19, 29

imperfect markets, 77
imperialism, 2
import ratio, 86, 93, 100, 104, 110,
114, 118, 126, 127, 133, 136
industry-specific, 108
inflows, 9, 15
intangible assets, 12, 17, 29, 47, 111
internalization, 13, 14, 16–19, 22, 27,
28, 45, 52, 64, 71, 72, 86, 105

internal markets, 13, 76, 77
international investment, 1
internationalization, 9, 11, 18, 27, 31,
68, 72, 76, 131, 133
international venturing, 108, 116,
123, 127
Inward FDI, 3

Japan, 8, 19, 47, 56, 67, 78, 80
Japanese, 8, 22, 23, 47– 49, 51–53,
55–57, 64–67, 72, 74, 77, 78,
80
Japanese subsidiary, 56
joint ventures, 2, 4, 6, 7, 75, 76, 84,
108–111, 132, 133, 135–137

knowledge transfer, 8, 45, 68–72, 84,
85, 93, 96, 100, 102, 104, 132,
134, 135, 139

locational advantages, 16, 17

macroeconomic, 22
majority-owned subsidiary, 97, 100
multinational corporations, 4, 5

OLI paradigm, 18, 19, 52, 72, 77,
137
outflows, 2, 9, 64, 68, 78
ownership advantages, 8, 17, 18, 65,
68, 73, 104, 111, 131, 133, 137,
138
ownership-specific, 18, 52

parent enterprises, 1, 5
parent firm, 6, 8, 68, 73, 75, 77, 78,
85, 96, 97, 102, 103, 106, 111,
118, 132, 136

portfolio investments, 1, 2, 11, 16
production costs, 13, 19, 109

resource-based theory, 30, 127, 131, 133
resource-based view, 29, 137, 138
restructuring, 22

sales growth, 3, 45, 46, 51–55, 62–66, 86, 93, 97, 112, 118, 126, 128, 131, 132, 134, 137, 139
shareholders, 5, 25, 86, 100, 107, 135, 137, 138
sophistication, 10, 23, 139
spillovers, 6, 9, 72
strategic alliances, 108
subcontracting, 2, 22, 24
subsidiaries, 4, 5, 7–10, 12, 21, 26, 28, 32, 45–47, 50–55, 58, 61–65

survival, 45, 46, 48–50, 52, 53, 55, 58, 61, 62, 64–66, 74, 132–134, 139

technology transfer, 8, 64, 69, 78, 109
transaction costs, 14, 27–29, 69, 108, 128, 131, 133, 136
transnational, 4, 5
transnational firm, 5

wholly owned, 24, 28, 49, 50, 54, 57, 58, 62, 64, 69, 72, 75, 80, 83, 84, 97, 100, 104, 107–110, 114, 115, 118, 124, 136
wholly-owned subsidiary, 54, 65, 68, 73–75, 84, 97, 100, 104, 105, 109, 113, 123, 127, 131, 132, 134, 136